TRAIL
RUNNING

TRAIL RUNNING

GRAEME HILDITCH

FROM START TO FINISH

BLOOMSBURY

LONDON · NEW DELHI · NEW YORK · SYDNEY

NOTE

While every effort has been made to ensure that the content of this book is as technically accurate and as sound as possible, neither the author nor the publishers can accept responsibility for any injury or loss sustained as a result of the use of this material.

Published by Bloomsbury Publishing Plc
50 Bedford Square
London WC1B 3DP
www.bloomsbury.com

First edition 2014

Acknowledgements

Cover photograph © Getty Images
Illustrations by Dave Gardner
Commissioning Editor: Charlotte Croft
Editor: Sarah Cole
Design: James Watson

This book is produced using paper that is made from wood grown in managed, sustainable forests. It is natural, renewable and recyclable. The logging and manufacturing processes conform to the environmental regulations of the country of origin.

Typeset in URW Grotesk by seagulls.net

Printed and bound in China by C&C Offset Printing Co

10 9 8 7 6 5 4 3 2 1

PICTURE CREDITS AND THANKS

The author would like to thank everyone who contributed their spectacular shots to this book, particularly those from the Great Trail Challenge for allowing him access on the course to capture shots of muddy trail runners.

Photography by Graeme Hilditch and Wigs Catto: pp. 8, 10, 11, 12, 17, 18, 19, 23, 24, 25, 26, 27, 29, 32, 35, 36, 37, 38, 40, 44–50, 53–64, 68, 70, 75, 78, 80, 82, 84, 91, 94–106 (top), 107–114, 116, 117, 120, 122, 126, 138 (left-hand side), 140 (top), 146, 148, 158, 168, 174, 176, 179, 181, 182, 183, 184, 186, 195, 204 (centre) and 205. Further photography: pp. 13, 14, 15, 20, 22, 33, 34, 42, 51, 67, 71, 83, 87, 89, 92, 106 (bottom), 118, 124, 127, 128, 130, 131, 133, 134, 140 (bottom), 141, 150, 151, 154, 156, 160, 166, 167, 170, 173, 177, 188, 190, 192, 196, 198 and 199 © Shutterstock; p. 138 © Tamara Kulikova/Shutterstock; pp. 34, 127, 133 and 134 © Viewranger; p.30 © Silva Ltd – www.silva.se; pp. 31, 136 and 222 © www.racingtheplanet.com; pp. 74, 77 and 218 © 2:09 Events; p. 209 © Jon Brooke/Dragon's Back Race™; pp. 206/07 (centre) © Le Champion; pp. 203 and 204 (left) © Eridge Park 10-Mile Trail Challenge; p. 219 (top) © Fuji Mountain Race; p. 219 (bottom) © Albatros Travel; p.213 (top) © Jumbo-Holdsworth Trail Race; pp. 200 and 206 © James Kirby; p. 210 © Mudrun; p. 220 © Jacques Marais; pp. 90, 143 and 214/215 © Australian Outback Marathon; p. 213 (bottom) © Rotorua Off-road Half Marathon; pp. 28, 115 and 216/217 © Routeburn Classic; p. 221 © Tusk Trust; p. 215 © Goat Adventure Run

CONTENTS

INTRODUCTION

"Don't fight the trail. Take what it gives you. Think easy, light, smooth and fast.

You start with easy, because if that's all you get, that's not so bad. Then work on light. Make it effortless, like you don't [care] how high the hill is or how far you've got to go.

When you've practised that so long that you forget you're practising, you work on making it smoooooooth. You won't have to worry about the last one – you get those three, and you'll be fast."

Micah True, 1954–2012

The passing of any iconic sporting hero is always sad, but the sudden and unexpected death of one of the world's most iconic trail runners was as much of a shock as it was a tragedy.

An outcast, an enigma and very much a legend of his sport, Micah True's way of life intrigued thousands of runners and seduced many more to take up the sport of trail running and explore remote parts of countryside. Although he took trail running to the extreme, often running over 50 miles of Mexico's most remote and unexplored trails without rest, Micah's passion for the beauty and serenity of the land has inspired many road runners to turn to off-road running and get a taste of the trails, Micah's lifeblood.

Sadly, it was Micah's unfailing obsession with extreme trail running that is believed to have ultimately lead to his passing. Although the exact cause is still a mystery, it is believed that a cardiomyopathy, a disease that results in the left

ventricle of the heart becoming enlarged, may well have contributed to his death.

Micah set off on a routine 12-mile run from Mexico to Arizona to visit his girlfriend, but never returned from the trail. After a major mountain rescue search his body was eventually discovered, his feet dangling in a stream. One of the people who found him stated there was no obvious sign of injury and that his lifeless body looked at peace, as though he had lain down for a nap and never woken up.

Although the trail-running community will grieve his loss for years to come, many will also be tempted to smile as they look back on his life, his legacy and one particular phrase he will now be remembered for: "If I get hurt or die, it's my own damn fault."

Although you'd be forgiven for thinking that this book is one long obituary to Micah True, this snapshot of his life serves to highlight the passion and freedom that trail running has to offer. The rawness and unparalleled freedom of running along a remote hillside or forest trail has the ability to lift your spirits more than any other running discipline, and it's this legacy that Micah True would have wanted to pass on to the rest of the running world. Micah True took trail running to its extremes, but the past decade has seen the sport of trail running change – and change very much for the better. Just a decade ago, when the popularity of recreational running began to skyrocket, the term 'trail running' was more closely associated with the likes of Micah – a hardcore brethren of runners who indulged in ultra-long distance, high-altitude running adventures, often in adverse weather conditions. In recent years, however, trail running has evolved into a far more accessible and less extreme form than it was once perceived.

Naturally, trail running purists maintain you're not a true trail runner until you've at least completed your first high altitude, rocky and rugged half marathon (at least) on a trail, but there is now a realisation among event organisers and health-conscious recreational runners that trail running needn't be extreme – just exhilarating and liberating.

Consequently, trail running has opened its arms to a new market and captured the hearts of new and seasoned road runners, all seeking a fresh endorphin rush from the challenges that off-road running presents. As a spritely 18-year-old, I discovered trail running's magic for myself and one particular experience will stay with me forever: a trail run in outback Australia as the sun is setting is beautiful in itself, but then I was joined by a dozen kangaroos hopping by my side as the landscape turned deep red, which became something special. I have learnt to really appreciate the memories this form of running can create.

Whatever type of runner you are – fast, slow, frequent or sporadic – you'll never regret leaving the asphalt and turning to the trails. Although trail running is best enjoyed when you have reached a level of fitness where you think nothing of running for a couple of hours plus, the trails are there to be explored and enjoyed by runners of all abilities.

This book has been written in such a way that you can dip in and out of it as you wish and flip to whichever chapter you need for inspiration and advice. Naturally there are similarities to conventional road running, but you'd be amazed at how just a few specific training and injury prevention tips can enhance your enjoyment of running on remote trail routes.

Trail running is there for every runner to enjoy and irrespective of whether you are new to running or already a seasoned trail runner, I hope this book will inspire you to continue enjoying trail running in nature for many years to come.

01

TRAIL AND ERROR

Taking your first intrepid steps into the world of trail running is an incredibly exciting time. Leaving the tarmac behind you, the trail paths and landscapes that off-road running can offer are as invigorating to the soul as running is itself. Take your time to embrace your surroundings and learn to appreciate what the trails have to offer.

Like any new sporting pursuit, it is learning from your mistakes, the many hours of practice and the time spent learning from others' experiences that will ultimately help you master your new discipline.

Trail running can take you from the muddy trails of the English countryside to the arid and rocky trails of California and New Mexico. Every trail you tackle will offer a unique challenge and even now, as a personal trainer and with many years and hundreds of trail miles under my belt, I feel I am still learning from others – and from the mistakes I make. Accept that your transition from road to trail will be a long process. Learning from every run and every type of weather condition Mother Nature can throw at you will make you a better trail runner – so enjoy the learning experience.

A NEW WORLD

Making the transition from road running to running trails can be a bit of shock to the system, so it's important that you accept it'll take time to adapt physically. Harder still, you'll need to learn to adopt a very different mentality to the challenges that trail running presents.

Trail running's ethos, philosophy and community are very different to those of road running, differences that are essential for you to embrace if you are to get maximum enjoyment from running off road and make a smooth transition into the trail-running community.

MAKING THE TRANSITION

Whatever surface you have spent the bulk of your running years training or competing on, the physiological action of running fundamentally

> ## LOVE THE ROAD, LOVE THE TRAILS
> It's worth pointing out, if it wasn't already obvious, that road running and trail running are not mutually exclusive forms of exercise. There is no reason why you can't combine your love of road running with experiments into the more rugged nature of trail running, but to do both successfully requires accepting that the two disciplines have their own identity – and part of the fun of venturing on to trails is discovering a whole new side to your sport!

remains the same. Although certain muscles are recruited and fire up at different rates when we jog, run or sprint, running is one of the most primeval movements the human body performs.

However, that's not to say that at a neuromuscular level it isn't complex or in need of 'tweaking' when you take to the trails, particularly when it comes to extreme ascents and descents. Running uphill or downhill, particularly at pace, does indeed place very different physiological demands on your lungs and legs, a difference that you'll need to master if you are to get the most out of the trails and your body.

KEEP IT SIMPLE

For such a seemingly basic human movement, and one which most of us have been able to do since the age of just two or younger, the actual (subconscious) physiology of running is incredibly complex, requiring a range of bodily systems to function simultaneously and in synergy to keep us moving, balanced and breathing.

The muscular, skeletal, cardiovascular, endocrine (hormonal) and nervous systems must all work together in harmony and complement each other, to ensure we can keep putting one foot in front of the other, mile after mile, hour after hour.

However, when it comes to running on uneven, muddy and undulating trails, the body has to make constant subtle adjustments in order to react to sudden changes in the texture of the road or

ABOUT ME AND MY RUNNING

I love being outside and I come from a small city in France where the forest is 50 metres from the doorstep. Whenever I needed to clear my mind, or just because I wanted to, I went out there. Being in the countryside makes me happy.

I really got into running when I moved to England two years ago; I needed something to keep fit, a reason to go out, to keep my stress level down. First I was running on road but then I found a park. I noticed that I enjoyed my runs more and could go for longer when I was off road. I like the feeling of freedom it gives me. It's a time just for me, when anything and everything makes me smile, from the little bird or squirrel to the nice colourful flowers in summer or the sound of the snow under my feet in winter. I just don't want to stop trail running. All these things are better than chocolate or a piece of cake!

Karrimor Great Trail Challenge was my first trail half marathon. It was really hard, the hills felt like climbing Everest but the feeling of achievement that you get when you cross the finish line is one of the best feelings ever and just for this I would do it again and again! I'm happy with the previous races I've done on road, but nothing compares to trail running.

Although it is hard it is definitely worth it!

>> *Laura Noailles – trail runner*

to change direction to avoid a tree stump or low-lying branch.

Although a few trail-running forum posts and articles over the years have tried to convince readers that in order to survive in the rugged world of trail running, you have to make major adjustments to your running gait, I do not believe those starting out in trail running need to become obsessed with dramatically changing their running style. Sure, for anyone who has spent the majority of their running years on pavements, paths or around urban areas, running on trails will certainly give you a very different feeling underfoot and you may need to tweak running elements as you encounter rocks, tree roots and almost vertical inclines/declines. However, the fundamental action of running should remain smooth, balanced, relaxed and controlled – resist the temptation to overthink and make unnecessary changes to your running action.

Despite the simplicity of the running action, you will need to ensure your musculature is able to tolerate mile after mile of undulating and uneven running. Strengthening muscles to help stabilise the pelvis, upper and lower legs as well as the ankles can help to prevent muscle and tendon strains and ultimately maximise your enjoyment of trail running for many years to come. There are a series of vital exercises you should perform on a regular basis to help prevent injury, which will be covered in more detail in Chapter 3.

In the meantime, my advice for your first few weeks of making the transition from the road to the trail is to simply follow Micah True's quote (see page 6). For now, all the tweaks you need to think about as you take your first steps off road and onto trails are to "Run easy, light and smooth" – the rest will take care of itself. The physical transition from roads to trails, even with these tweaks, is far easier than most runners think it'll be; it's the mental transition that many struggle with.

REDUCING STRIDE LENGTH

Perhaps the most important alteration you can make when you take to the trails is to reduce the length of your stride. The more complex and challenging the trail, the more control you need, so the shorter you can make your stride, the better. Most people transitioning from road to trail tend to overstride and find it difficult to negotiate tricky terrain, so keep your centre of gravity over your feet and reduce that stride length.

LEAVE THE SPLITS ON THE ROAD

It doesn't matter how long you have been running for, anyone who has ever taken part in a race, be it a 5k or marathon, will have been asked the same questions: "What was your time?" "What were your splits?" or "What's your PB?" The road-running community, rightly or wrongly, seem to have an obsession with speed, irrespective of whether you train for a road race with the view of completing or competing in it.

Recent years have seen huge advances in navigational technology, which has allowed time-obsessed road runners to make use of personal GPS systems and stride sensors to get real-time feedback of their pace, speed, mile/km splits, etc. As useful as this feedback can be when running on a consistent smooth surface, it becomes somewhat irrelevant and largely unnecessary when you take to the trails, and it's this very aspect that many new trail runners find difficult to get their heads around.

Naturally, as in any sport, there are plenty of opportunities to be competitive in trail running. When you feel ready there are a wide range of races, which allow you to test your off-road running skills against other runners. However, in the early days of your transition, racing and speed should not be at the forefront of your mind. Leave the splits on the road, keep your GPS device in your drawer and hit the trails with a very different mindset to the one you would take if you were pounding the pavements. Trail running is a far more spiritual experience than road running will ever be, so why obsess about how fast you can run to get off the trail, when you should be far more interested in spending as much time on it as possible?

TIME-BASED TRAILS

As a new trail runner, shifting your focus away from distance-based training runs to time-based sessions can be incredibly difficult and takes some getting

used to, but it's vital you understand the reasons behind this change in approach.

Firstly, every trail is different, so comparing the time it takes you to run one 10-mile trail route to another is pointless. If you obsess over beating your PB on every 10-mile trail you run, you'll soon become despondent, which totally misses the point of the trail-running experience. Trail running should be more about the environment you run in than the speed at which you can run through it, so slow down, forget about distance and enjoy the beauty of the trail and its surroundings.

Secondly, accurately measuring a trail route is incredibly difficult, bordering on impossible. Not only can GPS systems become next to worthless due to overhanging trees and dense undergrowth blocking the signal, thereby giving inaccurate

measurements, the same trail route can vary greatly from month to month. Felled trees, flood water and the racing line you take over a long trail route can change every time you run it, meaning you cannot rely on recorded times over an assumed set distance.

Think time – not distance.

EMBRACE YOUR SURROUNDINGS

For all the feel-good endorphins that a fast 10k road race can give you, nothing will be able to get close to the feeling you get running through stunning off-road scenery. You might find your first few runs frustrating as you mourn the absence of your Polar/Garmin GPS watch, but the stunning trails more

SHARE YOUR EXPERIENCES

If you think your local trails boast some of the best scenery a trail runner could possibly ask for, why not show it off to the world? The following places are ideal for sharing your trail-running images and experiences.

- **Twitter** – There are plenty of people and organisations to follow on Twitter where you can exchange ideas and share experiences. The following people are certainly worth checking out.
  - @TrailRunningMag
  - @TrailRunMag
  - @TrailRunningDay
  - @TrailRunningtv
  - @ScottJurek

  Start tweeting your pictures and you might even see fellow running enthusiasts from all over the world retweeting them.

- **Facebook** – By being an active member of a group, uploading your pictures on to Facebook is a great way to get comments from others and engage with fellow trail runners. The following Facebook pages might be worth 'liking'
  - Trail Running magazine UK
  - Trail running
  - Trail Running, from Runner's World
  - TRAIL & ULTRA TRAIL RUNNING

- **Magazines** – Most trail-running magazines are easy to contact (certainly by using Twitter and Facebook) and will be more than happy for you to send in your photos. If your images are good enough, they might even make it to print.

than make up for the (lack of) view of your mile splits on your GPS watch. Although you'll spend a certain amount of time fixated on the route ahead so as to successfully navigate around foliage, tree stumps, muddy bogs and rocks, there will be times when the landscape will open up to a vista that will take your breath away. Absorb it and reflect upon it. Incredible views are not exclusive to trail runners (I've seen many while road running), but there is a wider expectation and acceptance in trail-running circles that you stop and cherish the view before you – after all, it's not as though it'll affect your splits. Developing a love and appreciation of the landscape is part of what the sport of trail running is all about and there are a number of websites where you can post photos of your runs, allowing you to share your experiences with other trail runners all over the world.

PLANNING YOUR ROUTE

Until you get the real trail-running bug and start travelling long distances to seek out the best trails,

most of your training runs are likely to be on your doorstep.

Most of you will know of a forest trail, bridle path or foothill nearby where you can begin experimenting with trail running, but even on familiar routes close to home it is essential you plan your route and tell someone how long you think you'll take. Although I accept there's little risk you'll be faced with avoiding a 20-tonne articulated lorry on a bridle path, off-road running can present its own dangers, even close to home. A perfect example occurred while I was running with a client on a trail in the Cotswolds. The route around a beautiful lake was no more than half a mile away from his front door, yet while out on the trail he stepped on a hidden rock and twisted his ankle. The Grade 2 sprain left him in significant pain, with a very swollen ankle and unable to walk without assistance. Had I not been there to help him up and take him back home, he would have faced a very long and painful journey hobbling back on one leg – up a steep hill.

All this happened just a five-minute jog away from his home and the trail (other than one rogue buried rock) was far from extreme; it only takes a little bit of misfortune to find yourself in all kinds of trouble. Combine that predicament with inclement weather and no one nearby to help you and the consequences have the potential to be far more serious.

So, whenever you head out of the front door, even if it's just for a light 30-minute trail run, use the checklist on page 32.

PRE-RUN CHECKLIST
- Fully charged mobile phone.
- Map of the area, even if you are familiar with the surroundings (*see* chapter 8)
- Energy bar/electrolyte drink and water for warm trail runs
- A whistle

"I'LL BE BACK IN A BIT"

In February 2013, Sam Woodhead, an active 18-year-old from England on a gap year in Australia, got a little restless while working on a cattle ranch so he decided to go on a trail run. What was only meant to be a short jog turned out to be a three-day test of survival as he became disorientated and couldn't work out how to find his way back home. Taking just a litre of water with him, which he finished 90 minutes after starting his run, Sam fast became extremely dehydrated as he was exposed to temperatures of up to 40 degrees. He survived by drinking contact lens fluid and his own urine. He was eventually found by rescuers after three days out in the bush and only hours away from becoming critically ill. Sam was incredibly lucky. However, he wouldn't have needed to rely on luck had he been more prepared and taken a compass, small map of the area or GPS with him. This is a real-life example of how easy it is to get lost on the trails: do not let this happen to you.

- Bum bag with first aid essentials
- Bandages, adhesive tape, gauze, anti-inflammatories (tablets or cream), antiseptic cream, antihistimines,
- Tell someone your planned route and expected return time.

Once you get more confident on the trails and decide to travel further afield to explore trail routes in unfamiliar surroundings, the importance of this checklist cannot be underestimated. It is no

ABOUT ME

I never exercised – at school I hated PE, I left school went out to work, got married and had two children and still didn't exercise.

One day I decided we would enter a local fun run and run as a family. My two boys enjoyed the run, I struggled but still finished. As a result of this run, my son joined a local running club and every week I went along and stood watching him train until one of the runners asked me why didn't I run with them instead of standing around in the cold. This was the beginning of my love of running (or in my case, plodding!).

Since then I have attempted a lot of 10k road races and a couple of half marathons. I'm not a great runner and I'm usually found at the back of any race, but I have a go.

My sister is also a member of the running club and organised a ladies' training weekend away in the Lakes. I went along; we all stayed in a youth hostel for the weekend and we entered the Lakeland Trail Run, known as the "Sticky Toffee" run in Cartmel. Some of us ran the 10k, including me, and the rest ran the 18k. The night before the run we were given a talk on trail-running techniques; some of the advice made me wonder what on earth I had let myself in for by entering a trail run in the Lakes... I found out the very next day.

I finished the race after crawling up big hills, plodding across lots of muddy puddles and wading through a stream, feeling alive. Never before have I finished a race with the 'Am I finished already? I want to do that again!' feeling. I usually finish a race saying 'Never again!' I can honestly say I enjoyed every minute of it and the views were breathtaking. I have recently finished the Karrimor Great Trail Challenge 10k. I enjoyed every minute of it – the views from the fells were worth the climb alone.

I have decided not to enter more road races in the future but try to enter more trail runs – the views are much better and the feeling of achievement at the end is priceless. I would highly recommend trail running to anyone – just give it a go, watch where you are putting your feet, attack the obstacles and enjoy the views. The scenery is well worth the struggle to the finish line.

>> *Michelle Hedleley – trail runner convert*

exaggeration that any of these points could save your life, and although they will be unnecessary in 999 trail runs out of a 1000, it is not worth taking any chances and being unprepared.

For anyone coming from a 'career' in road running, these suggested precautions will no doubt sound unnecessary and even patronising, but it's a sad fact that every year trail runners all over the world get into difficulty miles away from home. You can be the most observant and balanced trail runner there is, but the trail should always be respected – it has the ability to take you down when you least expect it. Micah True is sadly testament to that.

PICK SOME BRAINS

No matter how many years you have been running, how many races you have under your belt or how

good you think you are at road running, when you turn your attention to trails, don't be afraid to ask for advice.

As a runner of many years myself, I am all too familiar with the typical Alpha male attitude of thinking you know everything there is to know about your hobby or sport. But the truth is, when it comes to making the transition from road to trail, you are only ever going to improve your ability, safety and knowledge if you accept the differences between the two, swallow your pride and seek advice from people with more experience on the trails than you. They may very well be less able, younger or lack your competitive instincts, but decades of road running won't give you the experience that just a few months of trail running can.

As with any sport, experienced trail runners are aware of the common mistakes many people make when trying out trail running for the first time. Rather than making the same mistakes as countless other newcomers, seek out seasoned runners who can offer you their words of wisdom. Even if you can learn one new thing, you'll be glad you asked and will already be one step closer to becoming an accomplished trail runner. Asking the right questions of the right people will hold you in incredibly good stead as you clock up the hours on those trails.

Although many of the following points will be covered later in the book, here are a few tips I have been given over the years, which I initially took for granted.

- Be aware of the difference a change in body angle can make to your comfort and performance when running up/downhill (*see* page 113).
- The right kit and footwear can make a huge difference to comfort in certain terrain and weather conditions (*see* chapter 2). Learn how to anticipate and adapt to sudden changes of ground conditions (*see* chapter 7).

by an errant tree stump, low blood sugar or general fatigue, then help is close at hand to see you back home safely. And as important as safety is, it's the banter of training in a group that is perhaps the most compelling reason to convince friends to join you in your trail-running exploits. Although I was joined by kangaroos on my dusk trail run in outback Australia, the experience would have been far more poignant had it been shared with friends. Running with a friend can make even the most innocuous experience last a lifetime: after all, falling flat on your face in a bog isn't remotely funny when you're on your own, but your running buddy will certainly see the funny side and no doubt tell an exaggerated version of the story for many years to come.

TWO'S COMPANY, THREE'S A LAUGH

Taking up a new challenge and learning it on the hop (especially if you are unable to seek advice) can often be a daunting experience, so there's no reason why you need to go it alone. The transition can be far more fun and exciting if you go through the experience with friends, so why not recruit a few chums to hit the trails with you?

There are several reasons why many experts positively encourage you to take to the trails in a group, but the two that top my list are safety and the banter/camaraderie.

The safety aspect of training with one or more people speaks for itself: if one of you is wiped out

02

KITTING UP FOR THE TRAILS

In the fashion-conscious world we live in, it'll come as no surprise that the amount of kit available to trail runners – whatever conditions you plan to run in – is endless. Whether most of that kit is necessary is a different matter. Strictly speaking, there's no reason why you can't hit the trails wearing just a pair of old trainers, a vest and a tatty pair of training pants, but there's no guarantee how long you'll last before you end up injured, hypothermic, sunburnt or (for the image conscious) laughed at.

The longer you hang out in the trail-running world and the more time you spend in the company of fellow trail runners, you'll discover a range of trail running kit. Some runners wear the cheapest and bare minimum of kit required to see them through their training regime and races, whereas others have all the gear known to man and feel bare without it. Ultimately, you have to do what you're comfortable with and what meets your specific requirements.

In the early days of transitioning to the trails, my advice regarding kit would be to stick with the essentials and, above all, make sure you are wearing the right kit to ensure your temperature is well regulated. Do your research and find the best quality kit to suit your needs and your budget. See later in this chapter for an overview of the different types of apparel to help regulate your temperature (see page 23).

QUALITY KIT – WISE OR WORTHLESS?

Will a £130 ($200) running jacket actually live up to the claims that its specially designed insulation material keeps you warm without the need for additional layers, or is this just a clever marketing tool to encourage you to spend over the odds for something you could actually do without? Often it can be very hard to tell, as the leading brands can sound incredibly convincing. The answer? Before you commit to a purchase do your research and, if possible, find reviews of the piece of kit you are interested in buying.

Starting out buying kit and finding a brand which you trust and that fits you well is often tricky, but once you know what suits you, it makes future purchases far easier.

The obvious limitation when deciding what kit to buy is the size of your wallet, so the best thing to do is set yourself a realistic budget and stick to it.

On the basis that you've probably come from the parallel world of road running, it's unlikely you'll actually need to buy very much to get you going – you'll have the trousers/shorts, which transfer well to the trails, and most long-sleeve tops are ideal.

Where you *will* have to spend some time and money, however, along with certain safety accessories and perhaps a weather-proof jacket, is on your trail shoes. These are a big investment and it's important you get it right. I explain more about choosing the right trail shoes a little later on (*see* page 27).

CAN YOU GO CHEAP?

If you are on a limited budget, then careful consideration must go into the kit you are buying. If you are torn between saving £10–20 ($15–30) on a running top/jacket or trousers or splashing the cash, you have to ask yourself whether you think it'll be worth it – going for the cheap option might mean spending a lot of trail miles in uncomfortable and poorly made kit, and you may well end up buying the higher quality product at a later date anyway. Quality clothes from quality brands feel good, often function fantastically well and will last you a good deal longer than cheaper alternatives. There are exceptions to every rule, but your running comfort is top priority when it comes to long-term enjoyment of the trails.

ON TOP

What you wear over your torso is arguably the most important apparel purchase you can make. Although our head emits a lot of heat, and we should cover it up in cold conditions, the heat we generate from our torso is significant through the course of a long run, meaning that our choice of clothing on a cold wintery trail or a hot and dusty one is vital for heat regulation.

WHATEVER YOUR BUDGET, WHATEVER YOU DO, AVOID WEARING COTTON

Cotton-rich materials hold on to sweat and don't let it go, meaning that throughout the course of your run your top not only gets heavier as it accumulates more sweat, but in cold conditions that retained

sweat can lead to heat loss. Any moisture close to your skin is quickly cooled by the wind, resulting in a dramatic drop in body temperature, which, although desirable in some instances, can be incredibly dangerous on long runs.

LAYER IT UP

Depending on the season, the climate you run in ultimately determines the number of layers you put on and the material of those layers in order to best keep your body temperature regulated.

In the peak of summer, less is clearly best to help keep you cool and a single mesh top or vest will do the job. Although considerations have to be made to reduce rubbing if you are wearing a backpack/

hydration pack, most vests are manufactured with comfort in mind, so you shouldn't have a problem.

In the winter, when temperatures can easily drop to well below zero, getting the balance right between too few and too many layers is difficult and often it's down to trial and error to help you find the right balance for you. When out running, we all produce very different amounts of body heat and therefore sweat, based on a range of factors such as running pace, running distance, complexity of the trail and our own physiology. If conditions are anywhere near freezing, follow the unofficial, unscientific, yet most widely used, 'Three Layer Rule' for cold weather training:

Layer 1: Base layer
A baser layer is a fitted sweat wicking top that is comfortable on the skin and helps move moisture away from the body. No matter how good the offer of cheap tops, **never use a cotton rich material as a base layer**.

Layer 2: Mid-layer
Over the base layer, a slightly looser fitting top offers most comfort. Like the base layer, it should also have sweat-wicking properties so that any moisture the base layer takes away from the skin and transfers to the mid-layer can be easily evaporated. High-visibility tops are often the best choice as you remain visible in dark or gloomy conditions. For runners who generate a lot of heat or for shorter tempo sessions, you may find that two layers are sufficient and you needn't wear a third.

Layer 3: Outer layer
The most appropriate outer layer is a weather-proof jacket, which helps to keep you dry and protects you from the wind. It also allows sweat to evaporate and circulates air around your body, keeping your temperature well regulated.

There are a wide range of outer layers available for different conditions. Some are very lightweight water- and wind-proof jackets, which don't do anything to retain heat but are excellent at keeping the wind out and making sure you stay dry in snow, sleet or freezing rain. Others have more insulating properties that help circulate air around the body while simultaneously providing you with good insulation from the cold weather. Running gilets/sleeveless vests are very good 'go-betweens' for

DO WHAT WORKS FOR YOU

Most of this won't be anything new to those runners who've faced all of Mother Nature's weather conditions, but remember that this is trail running, and the importance of your clothes becomes far more significant when you start spending entire afternoons or even days on the trails. Comfort is, of course, paramount but so too is the ability to stay at the right temperature for the conditions. Although the three layer rule helps to give you an idea, in cold conditions, trial and error is often the best way to discover what's right for you.

Tricky conditions to dress for are those which are in between – not freezing but not particularly warm either. In cases like this, accept that you might have to take off a layer mid-run and tie it around your waist or put it in your backpack. Do what's right for you, but above all do not be tempted to wear too many insulating layers. The idea of being nice and warm from your very first step is attractive, but this often means you'll be overheating after a few miles. This is not only quite uncomfortable and oppressive, but is also potentially dangerous for very long runs (*see* Chapter 9, page 137).

outer layers so they are well worth considering as a good all-rounder for winter and autumn running.

WICK AWAY THAT SWEAT

Any fabric close to your skin must ideally possess sweat-wicking properties, in that it must be able to take the sweat away from your skin and give it a chance to evaporate.

Most branded tops designed and marketed to runners are made of polypropylene or polyester and have sweat-wicking/moisture-transfer properties. They are easy to find online or in store and are often not particularly expensive, especially when you consider what they can offer.

In addition to their ability to take sweat away from the body and help regulate body temperature, they have the added benefit of being very soft, which can help reduce the uncomfortable condition of underarm chafing, which can often occur when wearing cotton.

Depending on the weather conditions, there are several types of tops and fabrics which can help take moisture away from your skin and encourage its evaporation. Mesh tops, or even part mesh tops, are popular choices in the summer as they are incredibly lightweight and offer you maximum moisture management. A word of warning though: If you plan to wear a back pack or hydration pack over a single top such as a long or short-sleeve T-shirt, ensure there are no protruding seams (as you'll likely see in cheap tops), which could lead to chafing due to the backpack rubbing them against your skin.

QUELL THE SMELL

Another good argument for you to spend a little more on a high-quality running top is that many have integrated anti-microbial technology; in short, they stop your tops from smelling.

Running apparel manufacturers use a range of methods to stop bacteria multiplying and making you smell, from silver, special salts and specially treated material. Silver, even in minute amounts, is an excellent element to kill bacteria – NASA have used it to purify water for years. If this additional feature of specialist running tops doesn't incentivise you to spend the extra money, particularly for your summer training, I guarantee your partner will have all your birthday and Christmas presents sorted for the next few years!

DOWN BELOW

Like tops, the season and weather you run in will determine what you wear on your bottom half, and although the heat produced from your legs is not as significant as that from your torso, choosing the wrong trousers or shorts for the conditions can make for a pretty uncomfortable and unpleasant run.

The vast majority of running trousers/pants are far less colourful than tops and simply serve their purpose, which is to cover the legs and protect them from the elements and aggressive foliage on certain trails. However, not wanting to be completely left out of the technology stakes, certain brands of running trousers boast performance-enhancing properties in the form of muscular compression.

COMPRESSION TIGHTS

Compression tights have hit the headlines in recent years and are very fashionable among professional and recreational runners. The theory is that by compressing the leg musculature during exercise, the tights can reduce muscular vibrations, thereby helping reduce fatigue and boost performance. There is also a theory that they reduce next-day muscle soreness.

A load of rubbish or cutting-edge clothing technology? The jury is still out. I wouldn't run people over in desperation to get the last pair in the store, but I'd certainly recommend giving them a go if you find them comfortable.

Other than compression tights, the majority of running trousers offer runners either full-length or three-quarter-length options and are mostly tight-fitting fabrics that wick sweat away from the legs.

RUNNING SHORTS

In the spring, summer and even autumn months, shorts or even short tights might be the preferred option to prevent overheating, especially for men. Courtesy of the generous allocation of hair on men's legs, they have their own in-built form of insulation, so often shorts can be worn even on fairly cool days.

The most important thing to get right when choosing shorts is the fit. Most shorts have an inner lining which helps aerate certain areas and wick away sweat. As useful as this is, if the fit of the short

is too small skin irritation can sometimes be felt on the inside of the upper thigh. This can lead to quite sore chafing and is an irritation you could really do without on a three-hour trail run, so it's always best to try shorts on *before* you hit the trails for some serious miles

RUNNING BRA

The importance of sports bras is often overlooked. Research conducted by leading sports bra manufacturer Moving Comfort discovered that a staggering 8 out of 10 women either wear the wrong sized bra or that it needs replacing.

Breast health when you're young might not appear to be affected by running for miles without adequate support, but over time, the stretching of the all-important Coopers ligament can eventually damage the breast.

Do not underestimate the importance of good breast support while clocking up the miles on the trails. Do your research and invest in a high-quality sports bra and change it as often as you change your running shoes.

TRAIL SHOES – GET A GRIP

As with road running, what you wear on your feet is a big deal when it comes to trail running, and choosing a pair of shoes to suit the terrain and running season is not an easy decision to make.

The difficulty of choosing a single pair of trail shoes is finding a pair that performs well on all types of trail surface. Unlike choosing shoes for road running, where the running surface will be fairly consistent (i.e., hard), the trail surfaces you'll be running on will vary greatly. Just some of the trail surfaces you may find yourself negotiating include:

- **Rocky:** Both small and large rocks will require a good level of grip.

- **Muddy:** Grip and waterproof shoes to tackle muddy trails are both considerations on this type of terrain.
- **Hilly:** Lightweight trail shoes might make hilly trails a little easier.
- **Tree roots:** Grip is essential to help you hold on to the trail and negotiate the maze of obstacles underfoot.

Consider the environment and trail surface you'll be running on most frequently when choosing trail shoes.

PUSH THE BOAT OUT

Most long-term trail runners have a pile of trail shoes they use for different conditions. If you're just starting out on the trails, my advice in the early stages of transition is to invest in one decent pair of shoes that are suitable for the trails you plan to be running on for the current time of year. When the season changes you may find that you need more grip, waterproofing or support, so it might be worth considering going shopping again.

WATERPROOF TRAIL SHOES

Waterproof trail shoes have been a bone of contention among trail runners ever since they

TRAIL SHOES DESIGNED BY THE KING OF THE TRAILS

As well as being a world famous ultra-marathoner, Scott Jurek is viewed by many as one of the world's most experienced and prolific trail runners. Due to his experience and competence on the trails, leading running company Brooks asked Scott for input into the new design of their flagship trail shoe, the Cascadia.

Critics of waterproof shoes often point out that as effective as they are at keeping the water out, if you step in a very deep puddle and allow water to enter the shoe at the opening, that water is unable to escape and evaporate, due to the very membrane which is designed to prevent water entering in the first place. This is a realistic scenario if you hit trails in very wet weather and you do not want to find yourself in this situation a few miles into a long run. My view is that if budget allows, it is well worth having a pair of waterproof trail shoes in your armoury; they are incredibly useful for snowy and damp conditions where water is present but not excessive, and they can very easily be used in dry conditions too.

NATURAL TRAIL RUNNING SHOES

In recent years, there has been an interest in more natural and minimalist running shoes for both the road and trails. The definition of what counts as a minimal or natural shoe is slightly blurred, but for the sake of argument they are essentially shoes that have far less cushioning on their sole. It is purported that this helps you to 'feel' the trail, offering a more natural run, while at the same time assisting your feet to run the way they were designed to rather than surrounded in the excessive cushioning most conventional running shoes offer.

Once again, personal choice must always be the leading factor, rather than powerful marketing campaigns and images. Due to huge variances in human biomechanics, we all run differently and our feet are happier in some running shoes than others. By all means try out a pair of minimalist running shoes but always listen to your body and if your feet don't agree with you and you find your lower leg muscles object, then either seek professional help or stop using the shoes altogether.

If you are familiar with the concept of natural running and intend to try it out on the trails, always

came on to the market. Some runners love them, while others hate them – but in the right conditions it's difficult to refute how useful they are. A special membrane coats these shoes, preventing water molecules from entering the shoe and, in so doing, keeps your feet bone dry. The membrane is also breathable, allowing for good airflow to your feet. Regardless of whether you step in a single rogue puddle or find yourself running through several hundred yards of flood water, waterproof trail shoes are incredibly effective and valued by trail runners who can't stand running with soggy feet.

TRAIL SHOE CHECKPOINTS

- **Grip:** Make sure the grip on the sole of the shoe is sufficient to meet the demands of your favoured trail surface.
- **Weight:** Trail shoes vary greatly in weight. This is a serious consideration if you plan to be running for long periods of time.
- **Breathability:** In hot trail running conditions, choosing a pair of highly breathable shoes is vital.
- **Colour:** The choice of colours available for trail shoes are infinite. Your choice of shoe should not be influenced by its colour, but it often can be – always choose shoe function and suitability over colour.

start off with short running distances to let your feet and legs get used to the different shoes and build up slowly.

MAKING THE RIGHT CHOICE

The best way to ensure you make the right choice of shoe is first to read reviews and then try on a few pairs. Like clothes, different running shoe brands suit different people, so put some on your feet and choose a pair that is both recommended by other runners and fits your feet like a glove.

ACCESSORIES

As a trail runner who is hoping to run in far more extreme conditions than you ever did on the roads, there are a range of trail-running accessories you should seriously think about purchasing. Although most of these accessories are useful for road running too, their necessity is increased when trail running, owing to the amount of time you'll be out on the trails and the fact you'll be encountering varied weather conditions and remote terrain. Here is a list of some of the most common items:

- Hat/cap – helps to keep the sun (or rain/snow) off the face.
- Gloves – extremities are prone to feeling the cold on long runs, so gloves are essential to keep your hands and fingers warm.
- Quality running socks to help prevent blisters. Double layered socks are excellent at helping to

prevent blisters as well as assisting in moving moisture away from the skin.

- Arm warmers – not popular with all runners, but they can help keep the arms warm without requiring an extra layer over the torso.
- Head torch for night/low visibility runs – the variability of the trail surface means that the more light you can shine on the path ahead the better. Head torches are excellent at dawn, dusk and night to give you maximum visibility.
- Reflective strips for night running – if you are running near roads, reflective strips are effective ways to let vehicles know you are there.

- Lightweight tent for multiday events – the range of these is extensive, so do your research and find the lightest and most convenient tent for your needs. Most races require you to carry your own kit, so investing in a lightweight backpack is also strongly advised.

SAFETY FIRST

Although your choice of clothing can contribute to your safety, particularly in extreme weather, here are some key pieces you should carry with you when you're out on a long run.

TOP FIVE SAFETY ESSENTIALS

Safety on the trails is a far bigger consideration than it is when running on the roads. The level of precaution you need to take very much depends on your knowledge of the local area, how technical or difficult your proposed trail run is and what type of weather conditions you are likely to face, but if in doubt, it's always better to be overcautious.

The following five items should be the first things you buy when you start to get serious.

1. BACKPACK/BUM BAG

Whichever storage device takes your fancy, it is vital that you get used to running with one or the other. Being able to store a range of nutritional, navigational and first-aid gear is key to your safety and provides comfort in knowing that if you're ever in a pickle, you'll have something that can help.

The type of bag you choose is very much up to you, but with the cost being upwards of £40 ($100) it's a choice you had better be sure about before you hand over your cash. If possible, before you commit to one, it's a good idea to borrow each kind from friends or a fellow trail runner and see which one you prefer – test-driving packs is by far the best way to help you make an informed decision.

2. FIRST-AID KIT

You'll be amazed at what first-aid essentials you

can squeeze into a small kit bag, and as you spend more time on the trails, you'll realise just why just a little first aid pack can give you a great deal of peace of mind.

The precise contents of a first-aid pack, to a degree, depend on environment, country and the conditions you are running in, but as a general guide you should make sure the following are always packed:

- Blister plasters
- Antiseptic spray/cream
- Small bandage to strap sprained ankles
- Swiss Army knife
- Tourniquet (just in case)
- Water purification tablets

HYDRATION PACKS

Some backpacks come with the option of a bladder, which can hold several litres of water/sports drink. These are known as hydration packs. This option is loved by some runners and disliked by others so try a few on and see if you are happy running with a few pounds of fluid on your back.

If you suffer from medical conditions such as diabetes, asthma, hay fever or allergies, it's important you pack all specific medication you may require while out running.

3. MOBILE PHONE

Although packing a mobile phone might be common sense, it's important to remember that mobile signals cannot always be picked up in the back of beyond. I've been on dozens of trail runs, in areas which are not particularly remote, and not been able to pick up any signal for hours.

That being said, just because there's a chance you won't be able to pick up a signal, doesn't mean you won't be able to. Even if a trail has intermittent access to mobile reception, that might be all you need to text or call for help in an emergency.

The recent evolution of smartphones has lead to much more versatile and lightweight devices. There are now a growing number of Android and iPhone apps which, signal dependent, can help track your run and give you highly accurate coordinates and satellite images of your location (*see* Chapter 8), potentially providing you with real-time and invaluable navigational data. This data is not only useful as a cross reference to track where you've been on your trail but is also extremely helpful in the event you'll need to provide the emergency services with an accurate location.

Due to variable mobile reception it's a good idea to check your mobile for a signal every 20–30 minutes and take a snapshot of your location and/ or coordinates. That way, if you get into trouble you can head back to the area where you had a signal as soon as possible.

Again, like many aspects of trail running, if you have come from road running these precautions might sound over the top, but trust me – it's good discipline to get into the habit of such practices. One day your cries of safety overkill

might just give occasion for you to eat a healthy dose of humble pie.

4. ORDNANCE SURVEY MAP

It may feel like GPS is squeezing out good old fashioned Ordnance Survey maps, but despite the obvious functionality of electronic navigational systems don't dismiss maps altogether. They're useful as a back up more than anything – and they never run out of battery.

Even if you don't consider yourself a highly competent map reader, it does not take long to pick up the basics. See Chapter 8 for a more detailed look into how a map can help your trail running endeavours and to learn a few essential compass skills to enhance your safety while out for long runs.

5. FLUIDS AND GELS

The early warning signs of dehydration and low blood sugar can creep up on you a lot faster than you might think, so it is important to take the correct precautions to counteract the effects of dehydration and hypoglycaemia, particularly if you're running in warm conditions. You can find more detailed advice about trail-running nutrition in Chapter 10, but for now it's worth making a mental note of the following.

As far as blood sugar levels are concerned, ultimately the best way to prevent them from dipping prematurely (i.e., after just an hour or so of running) is to ensure your consumption of carbohydrate-rich food is adequate in the days and hours leading up to your run. Carbohydrates provide approximately 70 per cent of your energy so if these stores are not stocked up before your run, you'll effectively be running on a half-full tank of gas before you've even stepped on to the trail.

Prevention is better than cure, but just because you've had a few hearty carbohydrate-rich meals in the lead up to a run it's still a good idea to have a few carb-rich snacks with you when you head out. There are a wide variety of glucose-rich gels or snack bars on the market, so choose a selection and keep them with you at all times.

As far as hydration is concerned (*see* Chapter 11 for more information), it goes without saying that the warmer the conditions, the more vigilant you need to be about your fluid consumption. On warm days out on the trails, you can lose well over a litre of fluid from your body every hour and if this is not replaced over a long training run, your performance will be dramatically impaired. Even if you begin your training run well hydrated, it is a good idea to ensure you take extra fluid with you to prevent dehydration. Some people argue that carrying extra fluid isn't necessary if you are running on a cold day or for less than an hour, but personally I think it's still wise to get into the habit of carrying fluid. Although there might not be a physiological reason to haul extra fluid on the trails, in cases of falls or accidents, having a litre or two of fluid with you is an essential, safety precaution and one you'd be very foolish to ignore.

There are three ways to carry fluid:

1. Hydration packs
2. Handheld running bottles
3. Bottles in a belt

1. Hydration packs Hydration packs are an incredibly useful piece of kit and are popular with many trail runners. That's not to say that everyone likes them, but their convenience and capacity (up to 3l) make them a good way to help you stay hydrated

on the trails.

Hydration packs are worn on your back, either as they are or inserted as a 'bladder' into your backpack. The fluid is delivered via a tube to just over your shoulder, so there's no need to break stride to take a swig.

Today, many hydration packs are manufactured to insulate the fluid inside, so your water or sports drink remains cool for several hours rather than slowly warming up from your body heat, making it pretty unpalatable after an hour or so of running.

While it's good to have enough water with you, 3l is around 5lb or 2kg of extra weight. So your legs are working harder which increases your workload and need for fluid! It'll get lighter as you drink, but do take the extra weight into account when you first try one out. Running on a tough trail for a couple of hours on a warm day is one thing, but running it carrying over 5lbs is another altogether.

FLUID THINKING

Unless you live in a climate which sees the mercury consistently in the high 20s (70°F+) throughout the year, chances are that many of your first trail runs will not be across great distances, so you won't need to take much, or any, additional fluid with you.

However, although you might not always *need* extra fluid while training, it's a good idea to get in the habit of running with fluid because as you get more proficient and the time you spend on the trails increases, you'll need to carry at least a litre of fluid with you on every run. So for the purposes of safety and practice, try to make a point of carrying at least 500–1,000ml of fluid with you on every training run.

2. Handheld running bottles

If you've made the crossover from road running and you're not familiar with hydration packs, then you'll certainly be familiar with running bottles.

Popular with endurance runners, these ergonomically designed bottles are made to ensure that fluid can be carried in the hand comfortably and with as little effort as possible.

These 0-shaped bottles can carry up to half a litre each and are ideal for trail runs in moderate temperatures for up to an hour – or a couple of hours if you carry two. The downside is that the heat of your hand can warm up the fluid inside quite quickly, so setting out with extra-cold fluid is advised – unless lukewarm water is your tipple of choice.

The main advantages to running bottles are that they are convenient to use, lightweight and cheap. However, if you are a heavy runner and tend to lose a lot of fluid when out on the trails, the 1l maximum capacity might not be sufficient for meeting your hydration demands.

3. Bottles in a belt

Conventional-shaped sports bottles may not be the best devices to carry for long runs, but when used in conjunction with bottle belts they can offer runners a compromise between the heavy yet high capacity properties of the hydration pack and the light yet low capacity of the ergonomic running bottles.

Bottle belts are a hugely convenient method of carrying fluid on training runs, giving you the option of carrying up to five bottles around your waist. Designed to keep the bottle securely fastened to the belt to help it stop 'flapping about', bottle belts offer runners the perfect balance of high carrying capacity and evenly distributed weight around the waist, ensuring running is comfortable while having easy access to fluid.

If in doubt, go for the cheap option and look on eBay for second-hand gear which might not be in perfect condition, but will be far cheaper than buying an expensive hydration pack or bottle belt only to discover you find it uncomfortable and cumbersome.

03

STABILITY AND AGILITY: GAIN AN EDGE

If you pass following the tests in this chapter with flying colours and show no signs of weakness or dysfunction, do not think you are out of the woods just yet. Although you might have good strength in all your hip stabilisers, it doesn't necessarily mean you'll also possess adequate amounts of flexibility in those muscles. Good strength is essential to help keep your pelvis and knees strong and supported during a tough trail run, but a lack of flexibility can also be problematic and a precursor to injury. So, if you cruise through the following tests and show no sign of stabiliser weakness, well done – but jump to Chapter 7 and check on your flexibility before you start celebrating.

Escapism is a natural human instinct and can help to clear the mind and put everything into perspective, so what better way to escape from the world than running on a forest or coastal trail and inhaling the sweet unpolluted air Mother Nature intended our lungs to breathe? Whatever the reasons for the upsurge of participants, it has resulted in a plethora of new events popping up all over the globe.

Many people entering trail events wouldn't consider themselves experts – trail running has reached a new market. For a sport once reserved for serious runners, its allure is now seducing thousands of new and novice runners to give it a go.

However, important as desire and ambition are, when taking up a new physical challenge the need for good musculoskeletal conditioning, as well as cardiovascular fitness, cannot be underestimated. As exciting as it is that more people are discovering trail running, many start their trail adventures with relatively unconditioned legs for off-road running.

MIND VS. BODY

Running for long distances on unstable and undulating surfaces is a significant shift in intensity for both the key workhorse muscles of your legs and the stabiliser muscles in your core, and running on

FORGIVING TRAILS?

One of the many reasons trails seduce runners away from pounding the roads is the far more forgiving nature of the surface. The often softer and more shock-absorbing nature of trail routes is widely regarded as a kinder surface to run on than the road and therefore far more forgiving on the ankle, knee and hip joints.

However, as true as this might be, it is worth noting that just because the surface you are running on is softer, it doesn't necessarily mean you'll be immune to injury. Undulating surfaces, hidden/slippery rocks and steep climbs can all put the muscles under a significant amount of tension as they are made to contract suddenly and violently. The softer and more forgiving surface may very well be kinder to your joints, but the trails can also throw plenty of potential hazards your way, so there is no room for complacency.

complex trails can cause a range of problems if your body isn't conditioned properly beforehand.

TRAIL CONDITIONING

Before the popularity of trail running skyrocketed, the majority of organised trail events were generally reserved for those who had been running off road all their life. Many successful runners, such as Bob Grantham and Kenny Stuart (from the Lake District, UK), were brought up running trails and fells so the need for off trail conditioning wasn't nearly as necessary. The thousands of miles they had put in over many years of running had automatically conditioned the leg and core musculature so the body was well adapted to coping with the demands that extreme ascents/descents present. That's not to say they wouldn't have benefited from further conditioning, but their training history and experience put their conditioning level far beyond the average office or sedentary worker who has just taken up the sport.

Whether you're looking to compete or complete it's a sad fact that if your body isn't conditioned properly for the trail, you risk injury. Poor tracking of the kneecap due to muscle imbalance of the quadriceps and weak gluteal muscles causing excessive stress on the knee joint are two classic causes of knee niggles that can creep up on you over time.

EMBRACING MODERN THOUGHT

Off-trail conditioning should play a major part in improving your stability and agility on the trails. Even if your philosophy towards trail running is geared more towards enjoyment than speed, performing a series of highly specific exercises will help to maximise your running enjoyment and hopefully keep you injury-free and on the trails for many years to come.

HIP AND PELVIC STABILISERS

There are lots of exercises you can do to protect against injury – essentially pre-hab exercises. Most runners could benefit from a series of muscle-specific exercises and drills to make sure they're well balanced for the trails.

The stabilising muscles of the hip and pelvis are key here – and these are the muscles we're going to focus on.

Although seemingly small and irrelevant, the group of deep muscles around your hips and pelvis are key to ensure a balanced running gait. If they are dysfunctional, weak or imbalanced, your injury time bomb will be ticking, so ensuring they are well conditioned is very much in your interest.

This chapter focuses on a range of highly specific tests and exercises, which will not only root out any weaknesses but will also offer solutions to strengthen them.

HIP AND PELVIC STABILISER TESTS

It is essential for lifelong, injury-free enjoyment of the trails that the muscles in your legs and backside interact with each other properly during every running stride. Although it's not immediately obvious, at a biomechanical level the normal functioning of these muscles is responsible for

SAFETY FIRST

If you are in any doubt as to how to perform these exercises properly or whether by performing them you could potentially aggravate a current injury or niggle (however minor), it's a good idea to seek advice from a fitness professional. These exercises are there to assist you with your trail running conditioning – not injure you – so if in doubt, please ask for professional guidance.

the quality of your running gait and ultimately the health of your joints. To ensure your key stabilising muscles are alive and kicking and doing the job they are supposed to be doing, perform the following tests by yourself or with the help of a friend to see if you need to do a bit of homework away from the trails.

The following tests will assess the function (or lack thereof) of the following muscles:

- Gluteus minimus and medius
- Gluteus maximus
- Lower stomach
- Obliques

GLUTEUS MINIMUS AND MEDIUS
Overview

Of all the hip stabiliser muscles, it is your **gluteus medius and minimus** which are arguably the most important of all. Situated at the side of your backside, in between your hip and pelvis, the gluteus medius and minimus play a number of roles in the stabilisation of the leg and pelvis and if weak, they can be the cause many injuries, particularly knee complaints. Injuries suffered by road runners as a result of weak gluteus medius and minimus are

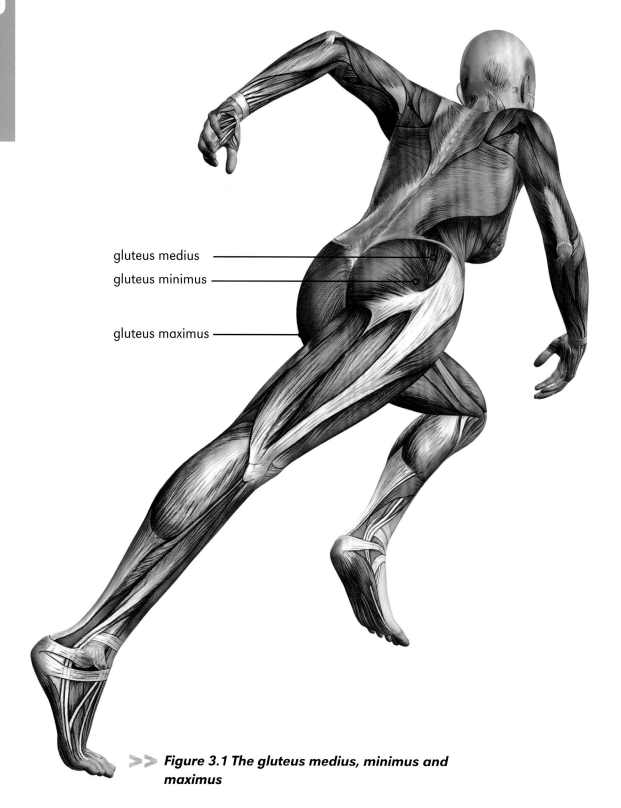

gluteus medius

gluteus minimus

gluteus maximus

>> *Figure 3.1 The gluteus medius, minimus and maximus*

common but the changeable surface experienced by runners on the trails makes it even more important that these muscles are strong and able to support your pelvis every time your foot hits the trail.

Actions

Strictly speaking, the functions of these two muscles are slightly different, although going into detail is beyond the scope of this book. As a trail runner wanting to prevent pelvic, hip and knee injuries, the main things you need to know about how the gluteus medius and minimus affect movement are:

- They abduct your leg, i.e., move it away from the body
- They medially rotate your leg, i.e., rotate it inwards

Importance

As many of us spend much of the day relatively inactive in front of a computer screen and/or in the car, our leg muscles can easily become inactive and weakened. The phrase use it or lose it could not be more apt. So what is the significance for running? How many times in the day, or even when out running, do we ever really need to perform the specific movements mentioned above? Your leg stays relatively straight as you progress through your gait cycle, so what benefit and purpose do these movements have in helping to prevent injury?

Reaction on contact

As we run and progress through the gait cycle, the muscles of the lower body work in a kinetic chain to ensure the legs maintain a smooth running action. However, if we have weak gluteus medius and minimus muscles on the left side, the right side – or both – the body compensates for this weakness by tilting the pelvis with every stride or turning the knee inwards, since these key bottom muscles lack the strength to keep the leg/pelvis stable. Over time, this pelvic tilt or inward movement of the knee can put pressure on a number of areas of the body, such as the sacroiliac joint in the back, the hips or the knees.

However, it is actually quite difficult to spot the weakness in yourself as the dysfunction is usually most obviously seen in the pelvis during running gait. When your only symptom is, for example, a knee niggle, and given that you can't see your pelvis or bottom when running, it's hardly surprising the last thing you suspect to be causing the pain is weak bum muscles. While there are a number of other potential factors that could be contributing to your niggling knee, if you play the percentages, the vast majority of the time it will be due to weak gluteus medius/minimus muscles.

Diagnosis

Thankfully, there are a number of ways to test for weak gluteus medius/minimus muscles, and you don't need to be a qualified physiotherapist or personal trainer to make the diagnosis. The simplest way to test the function and strength of these small but vital stabilising bottom muscles is in front of a mirror, wearing shorts or tight running trousers so that you can clearly see your knee and then perform the self tests on pages 44 and 46.

SELF-TEST 1: The single leg squat

Important: Perform this test before reading on.

ACTION

- Stand up straight facing a mirror.

- Very slowly, stand on one leg and slowly begin to squat down.

- It doesn't matter if you can't squat very far, just keep an eye on your knee during the movement and take a mental note of what it does.

- Repeat on both sides, only squatting as far as you feel comfortable but noting what your knee does on both sides as you progress through the squat.

ALTERNATIVES

This test can also be performed by doing a two-legged squat or even better, squatting then jumping on to a raised platform, such as a step. Again, just keep an eye on the knees and see what they do as you execute the squat as you take off and land.

SIGNS OF WEAKNESS

What did you notice as you progressed through the squat and more specifically what did your knee do the deeper you squatted?

YOU PASSED IF...

Your knee stayed relatively straight throughout the movement and didn't move inwards as you progressed through the squatting movement. The initial signs here are that both your gluteus medius/minimus muscles are firing up nicely and performing their job well.

YOU FAILED IF...

As you progressed through the squatting movement, you noticed that your knee instinctively moved inwards. If your gluteus medius and minimus muscles are strong and firing up properly they should contract as soon as you begin the squat and help to track your knee directly over your second toe (the one next to your big toe). As a general rule the further inwards your knee moves, the weaker and less functional the duo of your backside muscles is working, meaning that you've now got some work to do to strengthen them up to help reduce the pressure on your knees when you're out trail running.

Many runners are weak in this area, so do not think that you are alone. Your body is incredibly tolerant of dysfunction and although it finds ways to compensate for weak muscles, it's not a good idea to rely on the body to work around your weakness. You might be able to get away with weak stabiliser muscles for months or even years, but sooner or later the body will no longer be able to cope with the increased amount of stress that other parts of the body are having to endure to compensate for areas of weakness.

MIND OVER MATTER

When it comes to muscle testing and any form of postural analysis, the conscious mind has a big role to play if the testing is to be accurate. For example, if you have poor posture and know you have rounded shoulders, it's very easy to initially fool the therapist who is assessing your posture by simply pulling back your shoulders and giving the impression your posture is better than it actually is. Although most assessors will spot muscle tension and realise you are cheating, the fact remains that the mind can often help to deceive the examiner by overruling the weakened muscles and compensating by recruiting others.

In the same way as postural examinations, as effective as the leg squat test is for diagnosing weak stabiliser backside muscles, it is possible to cheat while performing the test, thereby giving a false negative result. Although cheating might not be intended, if you know that the normal tracking of your knee should be straight and over your second toe as you progress through the squat, it is possible to consciously fire up those weak stabiliser muscles and prevent the knee from presenting a test failure. Despite the fact that the conscious decision to keep the knee straight is one of the exercises to strengthen the stabilisers, it is not desirable when performing the test itself. So, when it comes to re-testing yourself after a few weeks of stabiliser strengthening tests, try to let your knee do what it wants to do rather than have your mind override it – it's difficult I know, but essential if you are to get an accurate re-test.

STRENGTHENING YOUR GLUTEUS MINIMUS
AND MEDIUS

There are many different exercises to strengthen up your gluteus minimus and medius – this is an easy and effective one to try at home.

EXERCISE 3.1 Side Clam

ACTION

- Lie on your side with your knees bent at 90 degrees.

- With your feet always staying in contact, hinge your knee up about 30 degrees or so.

- Always make sure it is your legs that move and **not** your waist.

- If you are very weak, you'll find that your waist will want to assist with the movement; do not let it under any circumstances.

- Perform 20 reps each side, three times.

- Perform this exercise at least 3–4 times a week.

SELF-TEST 2: Buddy up – treadmill test

This simple test can be performed on a treadmill with the help of a buddy and a video camera or smartphone. You can go out on the trail instead of a treadmill, but it's a little harder to spot what you need to look for, so if you have the option, a treadmill is preferable.

Unlike the single leg squat, this test requires no need for balance or consideration of what your knee does as you progress through the squat. All you need to do is run and let your buddy take care of the rest.

ACTION

- Hop on a treadmill and set the speed at a leisurely jogging pace.

- Make sure you are wearing a different colour top to your trousers (to help see your pelvis more clearly).

- Your training partner/friend should stand behind you with the recording device and, focusing on your waist and legs, record your gentle jog for 30 seconds or so before you step off the treadmill.

- If you wish to carry out this test on the trail, simply jog away from the video camera ensuring your buddy frames your waist and legs. Due to the fact that as you run away from the camera you will become smaller, the analysis may be more difficult, so it's a good idea to try it several times and choose the best one.

SIGNS OF WEAKNESS

The above images show significant weakness in the right gluteus medius and minimus muscles. As the right leg enters the stance phase of the running gait you can clearly see that the line of her blue top is fairly horizontal (1) and an initial analysis indicates that there are no significant signs of weakness anywhere. However, this shot was taken in the very early stages of the stance phase, just before the right leg and glutes took any significant pressure of the body as it continued through the gait cycle.

Less than half a second later, as the right leg and backside muscles take the weight of the body as it progresses through the gait cycle, take a look at what happens to the runner's waist at the bottom of her blue running top (2). It has dropped significantly – but why?

EXPLANATION

The hip stabiliser muscles on her right-hand side are required to stabilise the pelvis as her entire body weight is forced through her right leg and backside, but due to weakness they are simply not strong enough to support the pelvis and the rest of her body. As a result, her contralateral (opposite) side drops down in response to the weakness.

If you see anything similar when your run is analysed, and in particular if you failed the single leg squat test, this is confirmation that your pelvic stabiliser muscles need some serious attention if you are to keep on training and racing injury-free. It's not too late! After reading the rest of this chapter, check out all the exercises you can do to help strengthen your hip and pelvis stabilisers and cruise through the re-test of the single leg squat.

GLUTEUS MAXIMUS

Overview

Just around the corner from the gluteus minimus and medius lies the largest muscle in the human body: the gluteus maximus (buttocks). As well as being the largest, it can also stake a claim as being one of the strongest (although pound for pound there are a few others which could challenge for that position). In trail runners, for the majority of the time the gluteus maximus performs far less of a significant role as its size and potential power may suggest, but that is not to suggest for one moment that its role is insignificant.

Amazingly, the largest muscle in the human body is inactive in many runners and is not used as much as it should be. For a muscle that harnesses as much potential strength as the gluteus maximus, it is vital that all runners are aware of what role it plays during your running action and what exercises you can do to fire it up and get it contributing towards your power and assisting in stabilising your pelvis.

Action

The main buttock muscle has several actions, but its location and attachment points on the pelvis make it an excellent pelvic stabiliser, an important muscle to help propel the body forwards and fundamental in helping the body to maintain good posture in the trunk. In short, the gluteus maximus is responsible for the following key movement actions:

- Lateral rotation of the leg, i.e., rotating it outwards
- Extension of the leg, i.e., moving it backwards

Importance

In the same way that the gluteus minimus and medius muscles can become lazy and underused, so too can their bigger brother, and unless you are clear on what signs to look for, it can be very difficult to know if you are recruiting the muscles you should be when hitting the trails.

You'd be forgiven for not understanding why this weakness occurs. When your biggest and most powerful football player is ready to play a full game you don't put him on the subs bench, so why does your body let your glutes get away with not functioning? Unfortunately, your body is too smart for its own good; when your gluteus maximus becomes inhibited and fails to fire during exercise, your body automatically asks assisting muscles to up their game and contribute more towards helping to power your running stride. In the case of a lazy gluteus maximus muscle, it is the quadriceps and hamstring muscles that bear the brunt of the work as you clock up the miles on the trails.

All the while, your pelvis is suffering from a lack of stability, your running engine is missing a few hundred horse power and the hamstrings and quadriceps are working overtime to make up for the lack of glute contribution.

So, for all its clever compensatory systems, although you'll still be able to run the trails without proper functioning of the largest muscle in the body, you are exposing yourself to potential injury and are therefore unable to physiologically fulfil your potential as a runner.

Reaction on contact

Throughout a slow, flat and steady paced trail run on a relatively flat surface, when firing and fully functional, the gluteus maximus muscles coast along and assist in the background while the quadriceps (and other hip flexors), hamstrings and calves put in the majority of the work to propel the body forward. However, it is the glutes' role as stabilisers and shock absorbers during every running stride which makes them worth their weight in gold.

But their role isn't just limited to stabilisation – they are far more important than that. When the terrain suddenly changes, that is when they should spring to life and do some serious work. Arguably, it is for this reason that trail runners should be that much more vigilant about the function of their gluteus maximus than their road-running muscular counterparts.

Glutes are not your legs' key drivers during a long, steady-paced trail run on the flat, but when the trail steepens and you find yourself climbing a steady incline, with good running form you should be able to recruit your glutes, allowing them to take some of the pressure off the hamstrings to help you run strong up the hill. By maintaining an upright posture, as opposed to a slouched one bent over at the waist, your hamstrings become less burdened and your glutes should function and fire up as your legs drive you up the trail and into the clouds.

Complex and rugged trails with obstacles that appear from nowhere, such as large rocks/boulders, fallen tree trunks and streams, all need to be negotiated, and require your glutes to react quickly and be strong enough to tolerate a violent and sudden contraction.

Diagnosis

So, are you one of the very high percentage of runners who have weak and/or lazy glute muscles? Even if you passed the gluteus minimus and medius test, there is no guarantee that you'll pass the maximus one, so read on to find out.

SELF-TEST 3: Simple squat test

This test is an easy test to perform on your own and can give you a very good idea as to whether your gluteus maximus is what some therapists describe as 'overshadowed' and if you are 'quad dominant'.

ACTION

- Stand in front of a mirror, side on with a good posture.

- Slowly perform a simple squat, making sure you do not bend your knees any more than 90 degrees.

- When you have reached the bottom of the squat, note where your knees are in relation to your feet and slowly return to a standing position.

>> **An example of a good glute squat**

>> **An example of a poor, quad-dominant glute squat**

YOU PASSED IF...

During your squatting movement, you squatted as though you were trying to sit on an imaginary chair, with your backside moving backwards and your knees remaining over your ankle joints. This demonstrates (though a long way from painting the full picture about the function of your glutes) that you have adequate glute activation and are not instinctively dominated by overpowering quadriceps muscles.

YOU FAILED IF...

As you began your squatting movement, you had a natural tendency to put all of your body weight through your knees and as you progressed through the squat your knees found themselves well over the front of your feet. This demonstrates that you are 'quad dominant' and your quadriceps muscles, although awesomely strong, are overpowering your gluteus maximus muscle and making your body choose them over your glutes.

This dominance ultimately creates an imbalance in your gait. If you allow your quadriceps to do all the work while out running, your gluteus maximus will fail to fire up and come to your help when you really need it. By consistently relying on your quads they'll become excessively fatigued and you may even develop poor tracking of the knee, a quad muscle strain or tendonitis of the patella tendon – a painful inflammatory condition of the important tendon below your knee cap.

SELF-TEST 4: Buddy up – Glute poke test

Another very simple test to give you a good idea of whether you need to work on those glutes enlists the help of a trusted friend – and their finger.

ACTION

- Lie on your front with your head resting on your hands and your legs out straight.
- Keeping your legs straight, slowly raise one leg a few inches off the ground.
- While raised (extended), have your friend poke your gluteus maximus and your hamstrings, making a mental note which muscle is firmer.
- Repeat on the other side then swap over and repeat the test on your buddy.
- Exchange notes.

YOU PASSED IF...

When extending your leg, your buddy found that your glute muscles were as firm, if not firmer, than your hamstrings. This indicates that when you extend the leg, the gluteus maximus is well and truly fired up and able to contract when required.

YOU FAILED IF...

When you extended your leg, your glute muscles failed to firm up yet your hamstrings contracted strongly. This indicates that your glute muscles are not firing up properly and may be inhibited. This is not the end of the world as there are plenty of measures you can take to solve this problem, but it's certainly an issue you will need to address sooner or later.

BUTT BALANCE

Sometimes, just to complicate matters, you may find that after performing the glute poke test you notice one glute muscle appears to fire up and is more active than the other one. If this is the case, it is particularly important to work hard on ensuring the less active glute fires up to the same degree. Two weak and under-performing gluteus maximus muscles are bad news, but just one weak and under-performing glute muscle is even worse. Imbalance anywhere in the body, where one side is working harder than the other, is more likely to result in injury than both being inactive. The imbalance can cause excessive strain on certain joints and muscles and when the force becomes too much or has been prolonged, injury is the likely outcome. Common sites of injury as a result of muscular imbalance are the:

- sacroiliac joint (where the pelvis meets the lower back)
- hips and surrounding musculature (especially the tensor fascia latae (TFL) muscle)
- iliotibial band (tightness and resulting inflammation)
- knees and surrounding tendons

Muscular imbalance is not a friend of any athlete, particularly a long distance runner covering dozens of miles a week on uneven ground, so if you discover a muscular imbalance between your left and right gluteal muscles, address it as soon as you can.

If you discover that you have weak glutes, then performing the prone thigh raise exercise opposite is an excellent way to increase glute activation and increase strength.

EXPLANATION

The results from the simple squat test and the glute poke test potentially offer two different reasons why your gluteus maximus muscles are not working. As briefly explained earlier, if you failed the simple squat test and you found that your knees instinctively pushed forwards over the front of your feet as you progressed through the squat, it indicates your quadriceps are strong and over-dominating your relatively weak gluteus maximum muscles. If this is the only reason your glutes are not firing, then a series of simple, isolated glute-specific exercises are needed to both wake up and strengthen them, thereby taking the load off the quads and making you a more balanced runner.

However, if you failed the glute poke test and your backside failed to firm up during the leg extension when your buddy poked it, this is a strong indicator your gluteus maximus muscles are being inhibited by a series of muscles responsible for flexing the hips. Like all types of dysfunction, this is not an insurmountable problem at all but you are going to have to be religious about your off trail exercises if you want to reactivate those glutes and let them contribute to your trail running.

STRENGTHENING YOUR GLUTEUS MAXIMUS
The following exercise can be done at home and is very effective at firing up your glutes.

EXERCISE 3.2 Prone thigh raise

ACTION

To maximise the effectiveness of this exercise, stretch your hip flexor muscles well beforehand; if they are tight they can prevent the glute muscles from firing up. This is known as reciprocal inhibition and is a key player in many injuries. If opposing muscles to the ones you wish to use are tight, they can effectively switch them off, leading to overuse injuries of the other muscles which have to work harder to make up for the one which is reciprocally inhibited.

- Lie flat on your front, with your head resting on your hands.

- Bend one leg at the knee at 90 degrees, while keeping the other one still and straight.

- Without lifting any part of your pelvis off the ground, slowly raise the thigh of your bent leg off the ground a few inches, hold for a second or two, and then lower it back down.

- It's essential that you concentrate on using your bottom muscles to perform this exercise, as the hamstrings can also take over if you let them.

- Every time you lift your thigh concentrate on contracting your bottom and give the muscles a little squeeze at the top of the movement.

- Perform 15–20 repetitions, three times on each leg.

- Perform this exercise at least 3–4 times a week.

There is one more key muscle that you'll have to test. Will you make it a 100 per cent pass rate for all three tests or will you, as I suspect, need to be doing some more homework? It's time to find out!

LOWER STOMACH MUSCLES

Overview

To many trail runners, however experienced, the importance of strong and well-functioning lower abdominals is often seen as largely irrelevant. But while the integrity of the lower abdominals is not going to help you shave minutes off your times, a strong lower stomach certainly helps look after your back and keep your pelvis happy, regardless of how many miles you clock up on the trails.

Action

The lower abdominals' primary function for trail runners is to act as a stabiliser for the pelvis and back. If your lower abdominals are strong and contract when they should during your running gait, they will assist your gluteus maximus muscles in keeping the pelvis stable and ensuring you remain balanced, however challenging the trail may be.

Reaction on contact

If your lower abdominals are functioning well, you will not notice them working at all while you run. In a similar way that the gluteus maximus silently aids pelvic stability during running, so too do the lower abdominals, which contract every time your foot lands on the trail. The bracing of the lower abdominals helps with pelvic stabilisation and keeps your running gait balanced. However, if they are weak, your ability to stabilise the front of your pelvis during a run is severely diminished and back problems could very well be just around the corner.

Diagnosis

Finding out if you have weak lower stomach muscles and therefore have an inhibited ability to coordinate movement between your legs and your pelvis is very easy to do and equally as easy to rectify.

FACT OR FICTION?

Do your lower stomach muscles carry out a different function to the rest of your abdominals? The debate rumbles on. Some believe it's a myth and they don't work independently – others (especially therapists) stand by a series of specific lower abs exercises to rehabilitate people with lower back pain. Either way you need to pass the test outlined opposite with flying colours. If you don't then you have some form of abdominal weakness that will need strengthening.

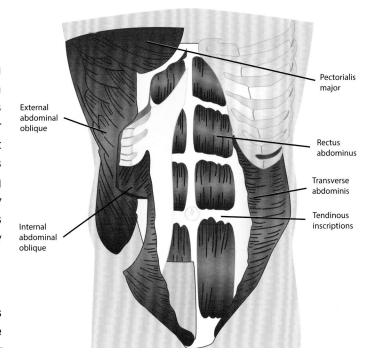

External abdominal oblique

Pectorialis major

Rectus abdominus

Transverse abdominis

Tendinous inscriptions

Internal abdominal oblique

>> *Figure 3.2 The abdominal muscles*

SELF-TEST 5: Leg drop test

This is the easiest test to check the function of your lower stomach muscles and there is no need for any apparatus other than a hand or two.

ACTION

- Lie flat on your back with your hips and knees bent at 90 degrees, so your lower legs are parallel to the floor.

- Place one or two hands in the lumbar curve (the small) of your back and slowly tilt your pelvis, so that you are applying pressure to your hands.

- Once you feel pressure on your hands, stop the rotation, relax your whole body, especially the shoulders as these tend to tense up when you first try this test.

- Keeping constant pressure on your hands from your hips, slowly begin to lower your legs towards the floor.

- It is vital that you maintain the same pressure on your hands during the movement of your legs. If you feel you are unable to maintain the pressure, you must stop immediately as continuing can place excessive stress on your lower back.

YOU PASSED IF...

You were able to lower your feet all the way to the floor while keeping the same pressure on your hands as your legs. This demonstrates that there is a working relationship between your legs and your pelvis. If you can lower your legs to the floor 10 times, all the while managing to maintain back pressure on your hands, then consider the relationship your legs have with your pelvis a very good one.

YOU FAILED IF...

You were unable to lower your legs to the floor without having to lift your back off your hands. The moment the pressure is unsustainable, regardless of how far you have lowered your legs, it demonstrates your lower stomach muscles are weak and have a poor working relationship with your legs. This ususally a result of a sedentary lifestyle. You will need to work on this or low back pain could easily spoil your trail running exploits.

STRENGTHENING YOUR LOWER ABDOMINALS

Attention to detail is the key to success in this exercise for the lower abdominal muscles. As easy as the following exercise might sound, many unconditioned trail runners find this exercise very difficult.

EXERCISE 3.3 Leg slides

ACTION

- Lie flat on your back with your knees bent at 90 degrees and your feet flat on the floor. It's best to perform this exercise without shoes.

- Place one hand in the small of your back and suck your belly button in.

- Slowly tilt your pelvis so that you apply pressure to your hands – not so hard that you cut off the blood supply.

- Start by sliding your feet away just a few inches where you'll likely find it hard work to keep the pressure of your lower back on your hands.

- If you feel your lower stomach begin to shake, good.

- Hold for 10 seconds and draw your feet back to the starting position.

- Repeat 5–8 times.

- As you get stronger you'll be able to straighten them further – something you should aim to do.

PROPRIOCEPTION – THE ULTIMATE STABILISER

As important as it is to fine-tune your glute muscles as part of your training, working on and improving your body's instinctive balance is equally relevant. Due to an incredibly intuitive system within the body, everyone has a natural ability to stay balanced on uneven surfaces, but when you're running on rough terrain at pace, this system needs to be honed and improved just like any other. The inbuilt ability to pick up messages from muscles and tendons and use those messages to balance properly is known as 'proprioception'.

Although many runners may have come across this term before, proprioception in my experience is something very few fully understand, so here is a brief overview of what it is, how you can improve it and ultimately how it can make you a better runner.

WHAT NEXT?

You should see steady progression as you address the weaknesses in the major muscles described above, but if you do not, there could be something else going on. Book yourself an appointment with a specialist physiotherapist to investigate further – remember, if you leave these niggling problems, they are highly likely to become much worse and could even lead to long-term injury.

CAN YOU STAND ON ONE FOOT?

Proprioception is one of those human functions which we rely on every day to keep us upright, balanced and functioning normally, yet we are oblivious to how reliant we are upon it, particularly when we are out running. In short, it is our brain's awareness of where we are in the world. The best way to get an idea of what it is about is to simply stand on one foot, without wearing any shoes or socks. What happens? If you have good proprioception, you shouldn't find that standing on one foot is particularly difficult; you can stand there without too much difficulty for quite a while without really having to think about it – but it's what is happening inside your body that's interesting. As calm as everything looks on the outside, deep inside your body, muscles and nerves are working overtime to keep you balanced, while the nervous system is working on the feedback it is receiving from your foot, making tiny muscular adjustments to prevent you from falling over. Watch the tendons in your foot as you stand on one leg – they fire up automatically without you having any conscious control over them.

TURN OUT THE LIGHTS

If you think you've got pretty good proprioception and are even able to stand on one leg while reading this book, that's all well and good but try it while closing your eyes and then see how good you are. Not easy is it?

Without any visual feedback, your brain is less able to know where you are in space and relies solely on your proprioceptive ability to keep you balanced. As a result, taking your vision out of play for some proprioceptive exercises can help heighten the feedback system your feet and legs relay to the nervous system and improve your overall stability and balance on the trails.

PROPRIOCEPTION TRAINING

Here are some simple exercises to improve your proprioception. They don't take long and most are very easy to perform – just five minutes or less a day is enough to encourage small adaptations and help make big differences to your stability on technical trails.

EXERCISE 3.4 Single leg hops

Single leg hops are probably the simplest and most accessible of proprioceptive drills. The best thing about them is you can add as many variations as you like to make it more difficult once you begin to notice your stability and balance is improving.

BEGINNERS

- Place a long piece of string, a pole or draw a chalk line on the ground.

- Stand on one leg about 3–4in (7–10cm) to the side of the line with a slightly flexed knee.

- Jump from one side of the line to the other on one leg, aiming to land equidistant on the other side of the line.

- Perform a total of 10 jumps (5 each side) on each leg, ensuring that every time you land you remain as balanced and as stable as possible.

- Once you are able to land on either side of the line comfortably and with minimal wobble, increase the number of jumps to a total of 20, and eventually 30.

INTERMEDIATE

- Instead of a straight line on the floor, use the string, pole or chalk line but this time form a cross, ensuring each line of the cross is approximately 18–24in (45–60cm) long.

- Stand on one leg at the south end of the cross with a slightly flexed knee.

- Jump to the north point of the cross, followed by the east point, then west, then return to the south, trying to make sure that every landing is as balanced as possible.

- Repeat this drill a total of five times on each leg.
- Make it harder by varying the challenge: repeat ten times on each leg, increase the speed of the drill, make the cross larger.
- Try randomising the jumping sequence instead of repeating the pattern north, east, west and south.

ADVANCED

- For the advanced floor-based single leg hop, replace the cross with a clock image on the floor.
- Place cups, stones, or any marker available on the floor at the 12 points of a clock. The clock should have a diameter of approximately 24–36in (60–90cm).

- Stand in the middle of the clock on one leg, your knee slightly bent, and jump to 12 p.m., then return to the centre of the clock. Then jump to 1 p.m. and back to the centre etc., until you complete a full 12 hours.
- Change legs and repeat.
- Once you are comfortable landing at each point and are able to land without significant wobble, challenge yourself further by repeating the 12 hours, this time anticlockwise.
- The ultimate challenge is to make the clock progressively bigger so that every jump is more like a leap. This will challenge both your proprioception and the anaerobic endurance of your leg and glute muscles.

DRILL VARIETY

We all know that variety is the spice of life and when it comes to proprioceptive drills, variety is key to ensuring your proprioceptive ability is challenged and conditioned for whatever the trails have in store for you. All the drills highlighted here can be built on and varied as much as you like, so do not be afraid to make your own tweaks or even create drills for yourself. Provided you are aware of the reasons why you are performing the drills and what you are trying to encourage the body to do, devising your own drills can be fun and a great challenge to put to your friends.

The ultimate challenge to your proprioception is to perform the drills **with your eyes closed**, but do not take this task lightly. Vision is one of the body's best forms of feedback for balance, so unsighted balance is incredibly difficult and should only be attempted on the easiest drills first.

EXERCISE 3.5 Stability disc drills

The use of highly specific proprioceptive equipment can add both variety and an extra dimension to your training drills. Balance discs and proprioceptive devices are easily available to buy, and most gyms also have a selection.

For the purpose of this book, I have included a selection of proprioception drills that can be performed on a BOSU™, one of the most versatile and widely available pieces of balance equipment in gyms and health centres.

BEGINNERS

- Place the BOSU™ flat side up with one foot in the centre, your knee slightly flexed. Some may find this difficult, so if you are struggling to balance, by all means start off with both feet on the BOSU™.

- Aim to stand on the BOSU™ for at least 30 seconds, trying to keep as stable as possible.

- Change legs and repeat three times on each leg.

- As you improve and you find that you are able to stand without wobbling, increase the length of time from 30 seconds to 1 minute.

- Once you have mastered 1 minute on the BOSU™ and can do it three times on each leg, move on to the intermediate drills.

INTERMEDIATE

- Once again, stand on the BOSU™ on one foot.

- Clasp your hands together and bring them up to chest level.

- Slowly begin to move your arms from side to side as shown in the pictures opposite, while ensuring you stay balanced.

- Initially, you will wobble like crazy as your

nervous system struggles to keep up with the speed at which your muscles need to react to keep you balanced, but over time it will get easier.

- Aim to complete 10 side-to-side movements initially, building up to 20.

- To further challenge yourself, perform the rotations holding a 3–5kg dumbbell.

- Once you have cracked this, it's time to really push yourself.

ADVANCED

- Assume your one-footed position on the BOSU™ again, which by now you should find pretty easy.

- Extend your other leg in front of you and place your hand on your hips.

- Slowly perform a single leg squat, ensuring your backside goes backwards and your knee does not come forwards over your foot.

- Initially you may only find it possible to squat a little way before you begin to lose balance, which is fine – just squat to a point where you feel in control, then return to a standing position.

- As your proprioceptive system adapts, you'll find you'll soon be able to squat lower and lower without excessive wobble.

- Aim to perform 10 squats on each leg, repeating three times.

ADVANCED PLUS

It is beyond the scope of this book to provide you with every BOSU™ exercise to help improve your proprioception and stability on the trails.

But now you have an understanding of how these drills can improve your balance you are in a good position to devise some yourself. The best way to work the BOSU™ into your training is to make the exercises as specific to running as possible. Good examples include:

- Lunges with your front foot stepping on to the the BOSU™

- Dynamic alternating lunges – fast lunges with the front foot landing on the BOSU™

- Lunge to hamstring curl with your front foot stepping onto the BOSU™

- Lateral lunge jumps

(a)

(b)

(c)

>> *Lunges on a BOSU: (a) standard lunges; (b) lunge to knee lift; (c) lateral lunge jumps.*

GAINING THAT EDGE

Hopefully this chapter has persuaded you that a few well chosen 'pre-hab' exercises can enhance your off-road running performance. I know how reluctant many runners are to squeeze in stability drills to their exercise routines, but just a few of these will help you fire up some lazy muscles to better tolerate the rigours of the trails. So, next time you are chilling out on the sofa in front of the TV when you could be doing a few simple proprioception drills, get up and get working!

04
PHYSIOLOGICAL DEMANDS OF TRAIL RUNNING

For all the human body's design flaws, the one thing they are incredibly well engineered for is running. Over tens of thousands of years, our bodies have slowly evolved, but when it comes to our physicality, it's clear that compared to other species humans are highly efficient at running incredibly long distances.

When it comes to endurance running, humans dominate any other species on the planet, so as you begin your quest for trail-running greatness it should be comforting to know that your body is designed incredibly well for the task in hand. Even the smallest and seemingly most irrelevant of physiological processes occurring in our bodies every day helps us to fulfil our primeval talents as exceptional endurance runners. Processes that happen automatically and ones that we have no conscious control over, such as sweating and increased respiration, all contribute to keeping the human body running whatever the conditions. With training, these processes can be honed and made even more efficient.

To highlight just a few examples of what is happening inside your body when you are out training or racing on the trails, take a look at the table on the next page and see just how amazing the human body is at making tiny adjustments, often at a cellular level, to keep you running and ultimately surviving. No matter how long, high, hot or cold the trail, your body will adapt to its environment in ways which continue to amaze scientists.

THE HUMAN MACHINE

Some of you may be looking for ways to improve your running efficiency for an upcoming trail event, while others may just be interested in learning how to improve your tolerance of hills, or others still may be simply seeking ways to adjust to the trails after making the transition from the road. Whatever category you fit into, I strongly believe that in order to improve or adapt to a new discipline or training regime, it is essential you understand as much about the running human body as possible.

Table 4.1 Physiological changes to the body during exercise

Physiological change	Effect on the body
Increased secretion of anti-diuretic hormone (ADH)	During exercise, specifically of long durations where a large amount of sweat is produced, the pituitary gland increases the production of ADH. This is an essential process as the increased ADH helps to promote the conservation of water within the body by increasing the rate of water absorption by the kidneys. By doing this, the body is able to reduce the amount of water in the urine, thereby minimising the fluid loss from the body and helping to prevent exercise induced dehydration. Without ADH we would dehydrate a lot faster, making less water available to the working muscles and causing a significant drop in performance, particularly in warm conditions.
Increased blood volume	Endurance training has the incredible effect of actually increasing the amount of blood in your body. Both the red blood cell count and the plasma volume of the blood increase even after relatively little training, resulting in a range of benefits for your trail running. An increased red blood cell count helps to increase the blood's ability to carry oxygen to the working muscles, resulting in better endurance and increased comfort on long-distance trail runs and you becoming more resistant to fatigue.
Increased capillary density in the muscles	As you clock up the miles, the working muscles of the body – particularly your leg muscles – undergo a gradual adaptation as they must learn to adjust to the demands being asked of them. Although they adapt in a number of ways to training, perhaps the most important process is the increased density of the capillaries, which feed blood and oxygen to the muscles. This increased density allows a greater exchange of gases, nutrients and unwanted by-products at a muscular level, helping to improve running performance and endurance.
Increased heart size	Like any hardworking muscle, the heart responds to training by increasing in size. This size increase is hugely beneficial to the endurance training adaptation process as the bigger the heart, the more blood it is able to eject with each beat. As a general guide, the fitter you are, the more efficient your heart muscle so it has less work to do at any given intensity. Over the course of a challenging trail run, this adaptation helps to conserve energy and assists you in running faster for longer.

By knowing why you need to perform certain types of training and what changes your body will go through in response, you gain a far better overall understanding about the hows and whys of basic training principles, which ultimately makes you a far better runner.

This chapter will help to give you a better working knowledge of what changes will occur during training:

- Musculoskeletal system
- Cardiovascular system
- Endocrine system

You'll learn how each system adapts to the trails and how you can tell if your body is responding well to the training stimulus, or if you need to make minor adjustments to encourage a greater fitness response.

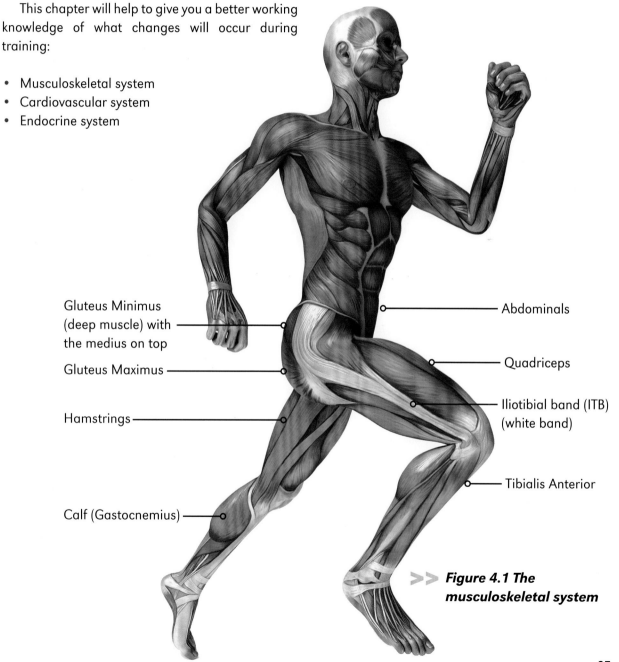

Gluteus Minimus (deep muscle) with the medius on top

Gluteus Maximus

Hamstrings

Calf (Gastocnemius)

Abdominals

Quadriceps

Iliotibial band (ITB) (white band)

Tibialis Anterior

>> *Figure 4.1 The musculoskeletal system*

MUSCULOSKELETAL SYSTEM

Comprising the skeleton, muscles, ligaments, cartilage and tendons, the musculoskeletal system will undergo huge adaptations throughout your training. Some of these adaptations will be noticeable, such as the improved tone of your leg musculature, and others will be invisible – but arguably far more significant.

The adaptations this incredible system goes through as you build up the miles on the trails have direct parallels with those made by training on the roads, but as you would have read in Chapter 3, the unpredictable demands of the trail surface means that the musculoskeletal system is taxed slightly differently – ankle muscles, for example, will need to be recruited incredibly quickly as the foot negotiates rocky terrain and a plethora of potentially ankle turning surfaces. Although subtle, it is important to understand the different stresses the musculoskeletal system experiences on the trails if you are to maximise your trail running potential.

ADAPTATIONS THROUGH TRAINING

Even on your very first training off-road run, the musculoskeletal system will sense the different conditions underfoot and fire up your upper and lower leg muscles to adapt to the terrain. Depending on how challenging the conditions are, if you are new to the trails and spend a decent length of time on them for your first run, there's every chance that the difference in running surface could give you surprisingly sore leg muscles for a few days. If you've been running regularly for years, you'll no doubt be familiar with the condition of delayed onset muscle soreness (DOMS), in which you suffer sore legs after a hard or long run. Even if your first trail run is not particularly far or hard going, your muscles will be undergoing extra work to negotiate the variable surface of the trail, which increases their usage as they are fired into life. The lower leg muscles are

>> *Trail running helps sculpt great muscles.*

particularly sensitive to this, so do not be alarmed if you show signs of acute shin splints or calf stiffness a few days after your first trail run, or even simply a more challenging run that you are used to.

As painful and frustrating as it can be trying to walk properly with lower leg DOMS, it is simply a process which the musculoskeletal system must go through in order to adapt to the trail environment. Until you have been trail running for several months, do not be surprised if your legs suffer several episodes of DOMS as you take on harder and steep trails. Your muscles simply have to adapt to the intensity of trail running.

FAST TWITCH AND SLOW TWITCH MUSCLE FIBRES

Conditioning the musculoskeletal system to endure the rigours of the trails takes time. However, through regular training on a variety of surfaces, every

LEARNING LEGS

Whenever you begin a new activity or sport such as golf or tennis have you noticed how difficult it is to perform the required movements? You need a lot of concentration and it can take lots of repetitions before your brain learns the correct neurological patterns to perform the desired action.

Over time your brain, nerves and muscles work as a team to learn the new pattern of movements – or engrams. It can take several weeks and many repetitions before a new engram becomes embedded. Once it is learned you don't need to concentrate so intently whenever the body is asked to perform that movement.

Trail running challenges your body more than the road running you might be used to – a way of running you haven't had to think much about since learning to walk and run as a toddler. But go off road and onto a highly complex trail with a maze of rocks, tree roots and water hazards and your running engram will be challenged to help navigate the new terrain. This is why you might feel more tired than you think you should and why even after a short trail run your DOMS are more severe than expected.

But don't worry – the more you train on trails, the more you teach your brain, nerves and legs how to react – your engram is tweaked and your body learns how to adapt.

run you embark on initiates a training response which encourages the working muscles to adapt to the stresses you have just put them under. This is particularly the case with the two (arguably three) different types of muscle fibres you have in your body – fast twitch fibres and slow twitch fibres. No matter what your level of competence, over the course of your training you will recruit both sets of muscle fibres at one time or another and it's how well you condition them during training that makes a significant difference as to how good a trail runner you will become.

Slow twitch fibres (Type 1)

When you head out of the front door and go for a long steady run, at a pace which is comfortable and easy to maintain for several miles, it is your slow twitch muscle fibres (now commonly referred to as 'Type 1' fibres) that are helping to power you

along. Highly vascular (very good blood supply) and highly efficient at converting energy from fat and carbohydrate, Type 1 fibres are the workhorse fibres of a long distance runner, and although certain fast twitch (Type 2) fibres come and help out during long runs, it is your Type 1 fibres which will see you through.

In most people, these fibres make up around half of the total amount, yet this figure varies greatly, particularly among well-trained endurance runners who have a far larger percentage – some even as high as 95 per cent. However, although genetics plays its part in your predominance of one type of fibre to another, endurance training has an incredibly significant role to play in making them more efficient. If your genetically acquired percentage of Type 1 fibres is lacking, your generous allowance of Type 2 fibres can be called upon and recruited to help out.

Fast twitch fibres (Type 2)

As their name might suggest, fast twitch fibres (more commonly referred to as 'Type 2' fibres) are recruited by the body when speed and instant movement is required. The body can call them into action incredibly quickly and they are vital for trail runners who need to take evasive or explosive action to hurdle a stream or jump up onto a boulder/felled tree. However, far from being a one trick pony, Type 2 fibres can also play a vital role in assisting the slow twitch fibres with the endurance side of running.

Type 2 fibres come in two forms. For years, these forms have been known as fast twitch As and fast twitch Bs, but in recent years sports scientists refer to them as Type 2A and Type 2X. Of the two, it is the Type 2As which are highly versatile and can help out wherever they are needed. Think of it like a soccer midfielder: they might not excel at either attack or defence, but they can help out in both roles whenever required. Type 2As work in a similar way for the trail runner. With endurance training, they can become a very useful partner to your Type 1 fibres and help provide you with energy when running intensity is prolonged or elevated.

On the trails, this specific muscle fibre recruitment is out of your conscious control, but with training you can adapt your muscle fibres to tolerate the demands of long-distance off-road running.

CAPILLARY ADAPTATION

Clocking up the miles and spending hours on the trails is essential to improving endurance and building up a tolerance in both the cardiovascular and musculoskeletal systems, but it's how the muscles adapt to such training that is fascinating.

Deep within your leg muscles there are networks of capillaries providing the legs with oxygen and nutrient-rich blood, which ultimately gives your legs the fuel to function and power you over the trails. Everyone has a capillary supply to their legs, from

CLEARING OUT THE BAD STUFF

Capillaries help to take away unwanted metabolic by-products, produced by the muscles during exercise. At low-intensity running, these by-products are relatively easy to get rid of, but when the trails get harder and more challenging on the legs, the extra capillaries are essential in helping to get rid of the unwanted by-products that can contribute to fatigue and lactic acid if they are not taken away from the muscles.

CARDIOVASCULAR SYSTEM

The cardiovascular system is one which we all, fitness obsessed or not, take for granted. It works tirelessly 24 hours a day, and unlike any mechanical system, the harder you work it the stronger it gets. So what makes the cardiovascular system so incredible and sets it aside from the other body systems?

- The world's hardest working and most resilient pump (the heart), which thinks nothing of beating over 10,000 times during a run.
- Two highly efficient organs (the lungs) capable of drawing in well over 120l of air every minute.

the couch potato to the elite athlete, but it is the density and number of those capillaries which essentially makes the difference between finding it difficult to run for the bus and being able to run over 20 miles of rough trail.

Through training, your body (or in this case specifically your legs) adapts to the stress it is put under in order to better tolerate the rigours of another long run. In the case of the capillaries, they adapt by increasing both in density and in number. This transformation is part of the reason why over time you suddenly find that a particular trail route you used to find difficult becomes far easier and by the end of the run your legs feel fresher and far less fatigued.

Through regular aerobic/long-distance training runs, it is thought the number of capillaries surrounding each muscle fibre can increase by up to 15 per cent. This increase in capillaries and resulting increase in oxygen and nutrients is clearly a vital physiological process, helping you to cope with increasing distances and taxing trail runs. Of course, you don't have direct control over the capillarisation process, so let your body make the capillaries, but encourage it to do so by taking on progressively longer trail runs at least once or twice a week.

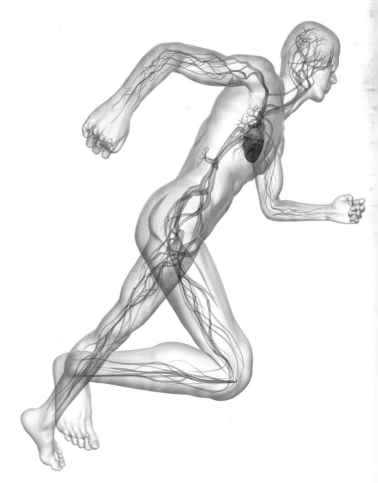

>> *Figure 4.2 The cardiovascular system*

- Over 8 pints of magical liquid (blood) which circulates energy-giving oxygen and nutrients to the hard-working muscles through a complex network of large and small tubes (arteries, veins and capillaries).

Working as a team, the individual components of the cardiovascular system come together not only to keep the body alive, but also to cover long distances on the trails. It truly is an incredible feature of the human machine and as a trail runner, you are going to have to spend the upcoming months conditioning and improving its efficiency to help it meet the demands of whatever altitude trail race: long, hard, cold, hot or high you have planned.

ADAPTATIONS THROUGH TRAINING

Sustained periods of aerobic exercise result in changes to your cardiovascular system. Your heart, lungs and your blood also adapt to help improve your tolerance to exercise. A few examples include:

- Your diaphragm and intercostal muscles (the ones between your ribs) increase in strength so that your chest cavity becomes larger and you can draw in more air every time you breathe.
- Your arteries become wider and increase in elasticity to prevent your blood pressure rising too high.
- More red blood cells are produced so that your blood can carry a greater volume of oxygen to your muscles and help keep your legs feeling fresh as you cover longer distances.
- An increased number of capillaries around the lungs mean that more oxygen can be taken in and used to fuel the demands of running and more carbon dioxide can be released from the blood to prevent a build-up of toxic metabolic by-products such as lactic acid.

Every training run you do will stimulate your body to adapt, making running the trails progressively easier.

The heart – the engine room

Of all the components of the cardiovascular system, it is the heart which is arguably the most important, and luckily it's one that we can monitor as part of any training regime.

The more you run, the stronger the heart muscle becomes and the more blood it is able to eject with every beat. This simple adaptation makes your heart far more efficient, as it has to work far less with every stride and every hill you encounter. The fitter you get and the stronger your heart, the easier those hills and challenging trails become as your heart is able to provide your leg muscles with all the blood they need to meet the demands of your run. A stronger heart means a lower heart rate, which ultimately helps to preserve your energy on the trails, making them easier and far more tolerable the further you run. Through training, your heart will adapt in a number of ways, with the major ones being:

- Increased stroke volume: More blood is ejected from the heart with every beat.
- Increased cardiac output: More blood is ejected by the heart every minute.
- Reduced resting and training heart rate: A result of a stronger heart and the consequence of the two above adaptations.

Being able to monitor the increased strength of the heart is an invaluable tool – Chapter 5 is dedicated to heart rate training – and shows you how effective a heart monitor training programme can be.

THE ENDOCRINE SYSTEM

Most people have some knowledge of how their muscles and cardiovascular system work – but the endocrine system tends to be the least understood. It is basically your hormonal system, and is very important to make you a better trail runner.

Your endocrine system is the governor of all your body systems and even if you have the lungs and heart of a horse, they will be useless unless your endocrine system is functioning properly.

Ultimately, without a fully functioning endocrine system your body will grind to a halt. However. the stimulus of hitting the trails will make it secrete different hormones at different rates, so that you can stay fresh on the trails for hours on end.

We have little control over the intricate functions of the endocrine system, which controls include:

- an increase in the amount of ADH during prolonged exercise to prevent dehydration
- an increase in the hormone EPO, which stimulates the production of red blood cells, thereby improving tolerance of sustained exercise
- the variable production of insulin to help regulate blood sugar levels
- the immediate secretion of the heart-stimulating hormone adrenaline, for those times you need instant/explosive energy (such as running away from a rogue bear!)

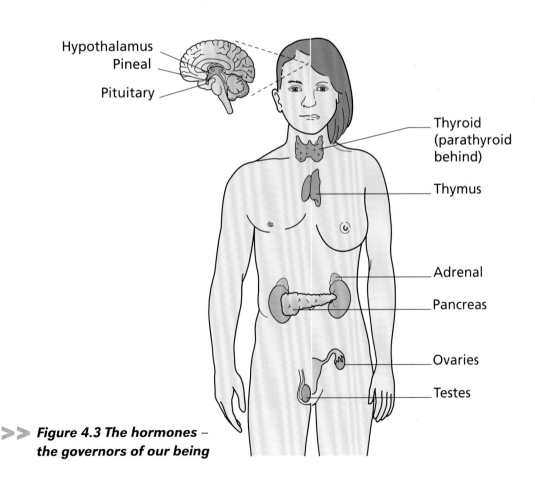

>> *Figure 4.3 The hormones –*
the governors of our being

All of these hormones and so many more play a vital role in your tolerance to training, and as your cardiovascular and musculoskeletal system adapt as you train, so too does your endocrine system.

FUNCTIONS OF KEY HORMONES
Let's look at our key hormones and what they do:

Anti-diuretic hormone (ADH)
The human body comprises 70 per cent water, so just a small drop in internal fluid levels through dehydration can have a massive impact on the performance of the running body. Although you might think you're the key influence in keeping the body hydrated by using that hydration pack

throughout your three-hour trail run, I'm afraid it's not a patch on what is going on inside your body to prevent dehydration. Thanks to a combination of signals within the brain, as your run makes you sweat more and you begin losing significant amounts of water, your body secretes increased amounts of ADH into the bloodstream. The increased levels of ADH are picked up by the kidneys, which act to retain water by increasing its reabsorption within the body. By reabsorbing more fluid, the amount of urine produced is significantly reduced, thereby helping the working body to retain essential water.

Without this function you wouldn't last any length of time on the trails or in warm or even temperate conditions. So next time you notice that your urine is

very dark in colour after a run, remember that ADH has played a significant role in helping you in your run and let this be the last time you are complacent about your fluid intake. If your urine is dark you need to take on more fluids.

Epinephrine and norepinephrine

Although the names are uncommon to most, you have probably heard of the more common name for epinephrine – adrenaline. Adrenaline and epinephrine work together in synergy and contribute significantly to the functioning of the cardiovascular and musculoskeletal systems. Most people are aware of the influence of adrenaline in situations of 'fight or flight', where a surge of adrenaline in the blood makes you highly alert and ready to take sudden or immediate physical activity, but it actually has far more properties than this. Together, adrenaline and norepinephrine have the following physiological effects on the body:

- Increased respiration
- Increased rate at which stored carbohydrate is converted to glucose for instant energy
- Increased metabolism
- Redirect blood away from the digestive system to the skeletal muscles
- Increased heart rate

From these points alone, it's clear to see that without these hormones we would never make it out of the front door, let alone to the start of the trail.

Erythropoietin (EPO)

Sadly, in recent years, this naturally occurring hormone secreted by the kidneys has been given a bad name due to its common use as a performance enhancing drug for endurance athletes. But as a trail runner trying to improve your endurance, EPO is a vital hormone as it increases your blood's

SLEEP WELL – RUN FASTER

The adrenal glands which sit behind the kidneys are key to performance, whether we are performing hill repeats, a three-hour trail at altitude or even running for a bus, relying on them to always function well is a very complacent ideology.

In the 21st century, our hectic lifestyles are packed full with stress, insufficient sleep and excessive amounts of adrenal stimulants such as coffee and energy drinks, which has a direct influence on the performance of the gland secreting hormones and ultimately affects our body. As a trail runner needing to call upon these hormones on every trail run you embark upon, it is vital that you reduce the amount of 'adrenal fatigue' you place on the body and ensure you eat well, drink low levels of adrenal stimulants and ensure you get enough sleep. There is a direct relationship between poor/reduced exercise performance and adrenal fatigue in the modern world and is it sadly fairly common among recreational fitness enthusiasts.

Adrenal fatigue is a condition where the adrenal glands do not secrete sufficient amounts of adrenal hormones which are responsible for normal energy production, heart rate and immune function.

Symptoms of adrenal fatigue include excessive tiredness, craving for caffeine or energy drinks and feeling run down or stressed.

So, in order to reduce your chances of fatiguing your adrenal glands and ensuring that you have sufficient adrenaline for training, try and heed the following advice:

- Get at least 8 hours' sleep a night.
- Reduce your intake of caffeinated drinks and do not drink caffeine after 3 p.m. as it stays in your bloodstream for at least six hours.
- Write down all the things that are causing you stress and deal with them as soon as you can. Stress is the leading cause of adrenal fatigue, so try to address your stressors frequently.

capacity to carry oxygen around the body, helping provide the hard working (Type 1) muscle fibres with all the oxygen they need to keep working for miles on end. It works by signalling to the bone marrow to produce more red blood cells and is therefore vital for the benefit of your cardiovascular endurance.

Unfortunately, EPO can be cloned in the lab and injected into humans to artificially manufacture very high levels of red blood cells, which have significant performance enhancing properties. Although high levels of EPO can be naturally stimulated by training at altitude, it's a sad fact that many endurance athletes have felt the need to cheat and have EPO injected rather than putting the work in at altitude to encourage the kidneys to produce it naturally.

05

RUN WITH THE HEART

Heart rate monitors have increased in popularity over recent years – but despite dramatic improvements in accuracy since the early days they are still ignored by many runners.

MONITORING CARDIOVASCULAR ADAPTATION

Despite their many benefits, lots of runners are either unfamiliar with heart rate monitors or choose to ignore them due to a dislike of integrating technology into their training regime. Although I always actively encourage runners to only do what they feel comfortable doing, I firmly believe that for trail runners heart rate monitors not only safely propel your fitness levels to new heights, but more importantly they serve as an essential health monitor. Let's face facts: trail running can be dangerous. Wherever you live, be it the UK, USA, Australia or South Africa, running into remote hills and woodland presents a number of physiological challenges to the body – especially in extreme weather conditions. Extremes of hot or cold have the potential to cause a severe drop in performance and health status if your nutrition is lacking or you simply spend longer out running than your body is trained for. By observing how hard your heart is working at any given moment, a heart monitor can give you early warning signs of any detrimental effects your training run or the environment is having on the body, so for the sake of your health, think twice before dismissing one as an unnecessary gadget.

We're all different, but a heart rate monitor tells you not only how hard you *are* working but, from a training perspective, can tell how hard you *should* be working. As important as it is to train hard to improve your cardiovascular fitness, training smart is far more important. For the benefit of your training and health, a heart rate monitor should be one of the first things you put on before you head out for a training run. It's a free world and you're welcome to disagree, but I hope the following chapter will help to change your mind.

LISTEN TO YOUR HEART

The fundamental principle of endurance training is that you have to overload your body to tolerate

the demands of what you are asking it to do. However, the secret to building good endurance is to remember that as important as training **quantity** is, the actual **quality** of your training should never be underestimated. Although the quality of your sessions derive from several aspects of training, such as running form, technique and specificity, by training in accordance with suggested heart rate zones, you can ensure you are running at the right pace 100 per cent of the time. If you are training for an undulating half marathon in a few months' time, you should be encouraging your heart and legs to adapt to the expected conditions on race day. By using a heart rate monitor to work within these boundaries, you can train your legs, lungs and heart at the ideal intensity for every training session without running the risk of pushing yourself too hard – or not hard enough. After several weeks and months of hilly trail runs performed at the right intensity, the musculature of your legs and your heart will have adapted perfectly to expected race conditions and you'll gain the performance you expect of them come race day.

BUYING A HEART RATE MONITOR

There are a wide range of heart monitors on the market. Some include the basic functions such as the time spent exercising and current heart rate right up to monitors that chart your pace via GPS, your current and average heart rate.

All monitors come with a heart rate strap that allows you to fasten it around your chest (below the chest muscles) and a watch receiver, though many smart phones can also pick up heart rate if you wear a Bluetooth heart rate strap.

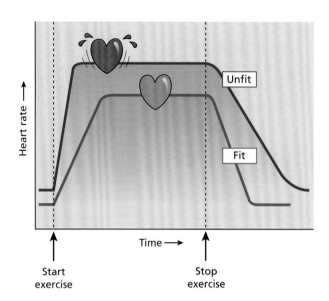

Figure 5.1 Heart rate graph

MONITORING YOUR TRAINING ZONE

A heart rate monitor can give you a very accurate idea of how your heart is adapting to your training runs and, short of taking blood samples from your legs to determine lactic acid levels, it's the most accurate and convenient feedback you can obtain.

Figure 5.1 is a typical example of how the heart rate of an unfit runner versus a fit runner running on the flat changes and adapts to the demands of regular endurance training over a period of months.

As the graph clearly shows, the unconditioned runner is far less able to cope with the high demands of exercise and therefore has to work incredibly hard in order to meet the speed and energy demands asked of his body. As his heart rate soars and nears its maximal capacity, his body finds it increasingly more difficult to clear the metabolic waste products, produced by the hard-working leg muscles, from the blood. Eventually, unless his heart rate drops, fatigue will set in and he'll be forced to stop, as he'll simply be unable to continue running at that intensity.

Imagine what the graph would look like if you compared two trail runners with different levels of fitness. Throw in some inclines, an uneven trail, a few jumps and the weight of a backpack and that heart rate graph will be going crazy. And so will your heart if you're not conditioned for the trail. This is where using a heart rate monitor has its greatest rewards; it provides information about the state of your heart and how well adapted it is (currently) to trail running. Although the only feedback you will receive from your monitor will be numbers ranging from 100 to 200, by the end of this chapter you will learn how to translate the information it is giving you. This will include:

- if your heart rate is too high for a certain distanced trail
- how well your heart is able to recover from sudden increases in intensity
- how well your heart can tolerate sustained inclines
- if you could actually push yourself a little harder

CALCULATING YOUR HEART RATE TRAINING ZONE

Despite the potential benefits that heart rate training can contribute to your overall fitness, using the heart monitor the way it is intended is vital. Over the years, I have seen far too many people enthusiastically use their heart rate monitor on a training run yet be clueless as to whether they are actually training at the right intensity. As runners, we are all built differently and the ways our hearts respond to training vary massively from person to person. The mistake many runners make when they first start using a heart rate monitor is copying the heart rate of a friend, which might turn out to be suitable, but could also be disastrous.

To avoid either working excessively hard during a steady trail run or not working hard enough, you need to work out your true maximum heart rate.

>> *Calculating your heart rate zone*

From this figure, you can then work out how hard your heart should be working for any given intensity of training session you run.

HEART RATE MAX

Commonly abbreviated to HR max, working out your true (as opposed to theoretical) maximum heart rate is essential if you are to rely on heart rate training to help improve your trail running fitness.

Over the years, you will no doubt have come across training articles suggesting that the most practical method of working out your maximum heart rate is to use the simple formula of subtracting your age from 220. Practical maybe, but this formula is often very inaccurate and generally regarded by most fitness professionals as an unreliable method of predicting your HR max. To get a true idea of your HR max I'm afraid you'll need to put yourself through something a little more taxing than primary school maths. By all means use the '220 minus your age' formula as a guide, but if you are serious about your training and want the peace of mind that you will always be training at the correct intensity, you'll need to undergo a maximal exercise test to see what level your heart can reach.

There are several ways you can perform a maximal test, so choose the one you feel is most convenient for you, and if you fancy trying another test at a later date, by all means go for it.

MAXIMUM HEART RATE TESTS
Test 1: Progressive treadmill test

- Step onto the treadmill (on incline 1) and jog gently for 10–15 minutes to warm up, gradually increasing the pace.
- Hop off and stretch thoroughly, then get ready for a tough workout.

- Begin the workout on a very low speed and increase the speed by 1kph every 2 minutes.
- If possible, have a friend chart your heart at the end of every 2-minute level. A comfortable strap can be fastened around your chest and a friend can monitor your heart rate by simply holding the receiver (watch or smart phone) near you. Different monitors can detect different ranges but most heart rates can be picked up within 4–5 feet.
- Keep running until you cannot run any further – this is often further than you think so really put 100 per cent effort into the test.
- The following example shows you what a typical test might look like (*see* table 5.1 below).
- Towards the end of the test, your heart rate will begin to plateau at the end of every speed – this is normal and indicates that you are nearing your maximum heart rate.

Provided you have put 100 per cent effort into the test and have nothing left to give, the heart rate

Table 5.1 Speed vs. heart rate

Speed (kph)	Heart rate
8	110
9	122
10	134
11	144
12	155
13	165
14	173
15	176

ROAD HEART RATE VS. TRAIL HEART RATE

For those of you who have used a heart rate monitor before while road running, it is worth remembering that you cannot translate your road heart rate directly to your trail heart rate. Due to the variation of conditions underfoot, you will experience sudden increases in your heart rate followed by sudden decreases. By comparison, your heart rate on the road will be smoother and with fewer spikes due to the more gradual nature of the topography. As a result, always bear in mind that unlike road running, where it's generally fairly easy to stay in your heart rate zones, while out on the trails your heart rate will often stray outside your suggested zone, albeit temporarily. This is fully expected and is part of the beauty of trail running – the variability of the running surface always keeps you on your toes. Provided your heart rate drops back down into the correct training zone a few moments after a sudden spike upon encountering a sharp incline, there is no need to adjust your running speed in an effort to religiously stay in your training zone.

you finish on is your maximum heart rate. Although there's a chance that you might be able to squeeze an extra beat or two out, this method is still very accurate and a good figure for you to use when working out your heart rate zones.

Test 2: Trail-running test

If the idea of spending wasted running time on the treadmill rather than out on the trails freaks you out, fear not, as there is another test you can do while out running. It may not give you such an accurate reading but it'll likely still be far more accurate than the 220 minus your age formula.

- Plan a decent length trail run of around 45–60 minutes.
- Begin your run as you normally would at a steady pace, checking your heart rate regularly.
- 15–20 minutes before the end of the run, begin to pick up your pace ever so slightly every minute or so.
- Each passing minute, continue to speed up until going nearly all out for the last couple of minutes.

- Put 100 per cent effort into the closing minutes and keep running until you feel it is physically impossible to continue.
- The heart rate reading you finish on is your maximum heart rate.

TRAIL TRAINING ZONES

Once you have an accurate HR max to work with, you can now start working out what heart training zones you should be working in for any given training session you take on. By training in specific heart rate zones for every training run, you can make sure that you are training at the right intensity at any given time, irrespective of the type of training session you are doing. By looking at the number of beats on your heart rate monitor, you will be able to tell in an instant if you are under-pacing and not overloading the body sufficiently to increase fitness levels, or over-pacing and running the risk of premature fatigue.

DEFINING TRAINING ZONES

Armed with your true maximum heart rate, you are now in a position to work out how hard your heart

Table 5.2 Heart rate training zones

% HR Max	Heart rate (bpm)	Training session	Expected overspill from sudden inclines
70–85%	126–153	Steady training run	10–15bpm
85–90%	153–162	Tempo run	5–10bpm
90–100%	162–180	Hills/intervals	2–5bpm

should be beating depending on the intensity of training session you wish to attempt. Examples of various training sessions may include:

- Steady/long distance training run – **70–85% HR max** (moderate intensity)
- Tempo training run – **85–90% HR max** (high intensity)
- Hill training session – **90–100% HR max** (very high intensity)
- Interval training session – **90–100% HR max** (very high intensity)

LEAPS AND BOUNDS

If you are still fairly new to running and feel unconditioned for the trails, keep a close eye on how your heart rate responds to training for the first few weeks. You will notice significant changes in your resting and active heart rate as your heart slowly becomes stronger and adapts to tolerate the longer distances and faster pace.

Although I recommend that all runners re-evaluate their heart rate zones every few weeks, if you still consider yourself a novice runner, this re-evaluation is particularly important as you will notice far greater variability week on week.

In terms of heart rate, if we work on an example of someone with a maximum heart rate of 180 beats per minute (bpm), these sessions can be determined by the following heart rate zones.

HEART RATE VARIABILITY

Unfortunately, like training itself, heart rate training in not an exact science. Due to the variability of the human body and everyone's slightly different tolerances to training, as effective as running in tune with your heart can be, it is important that you are aware there is no rule book to adhere to; rather it is a guide book. The examples of the heart rate zones above can be useful to give you a good idea of how hard you should be training, but as you get more familiar with your body and how it responds and feels running at certain intensities, you have licence to amend your training zones accordingly. Human individuality, improvements in fitness and even training history can have a massive influence on how your heart responds to training, so if you feel very comfortable on your steady runs with a heart rate at a higher or lower percentage HR max than that which is suggested, use your instincts and adjust your zones. Equally, if you are tiring after just 45 minutes into a 90-minute run with a heart rate of 75 per cent, feel free to reduce your pace and run at a 65–70% HR Max pace. Train within your means and, above all, always listen to *your* body and no one else's.

DEAR DIARY...

Putting the hours and miles in on the trails and collecting heart rate data is all well and good but using that data effectively to chart your fitness improvements is essential if you are to unlock the true potential of heart rate training.

From your very first day of wearing a heart rate monitor, I strongly suggest you get into the habit of keeping a running diary and write down specific pieces of information immediately after your run. If you have invested in a top range heart monitor, you will have the option to upload your training run data onto your computer where it will automatically record everything from the time on the trail, your average heart rate and even the route you ran (provided you have GPS functionality). However if you choose to record your training information, you should make sure you keep note of the following:

- Date of training run
- Distance or your name for the trail route, i.e., Short loop in Sycamore Wood
- Ambient temperature
- Time it took
- Average heart rate for the run
- Maximum heart rate for the run
- How you felt during the run

Logging training run information is essential for keeping track of your fitness improvements. The data you enter may not necessarily change on a weekly basis, but over the course of a month or two you'll notice a big difference when you compare the data for the same training run. Provided you train consistently and adhere to the training guidelines in Chapter 7, give it a few months and the entries on the following page will look very familiar:

>> *Charting your running progress is vital.*

1 May 2012	15 July 2012
10-mile trail near the old railway	10-mile trail near the old railway
22 degrees	23 degrees
93 minutes	86 minutes
Av. HR 160	Av. HR 153
Max HR 184	Max HR 177
Felt okay for most, but tired for last 3 miles	Felt pretty easy, could have gone quicker

Depending on how well your body adapts to the rigours of training, not only can you expect a lower heart rate for the same training run performed at a similar speed, but there is every chance that you will even notice a lower average heart rate even if you run the route several minutes faster.

A diary like this is not just suitable for logging data for long-distance training runs, but also hill intervals and speed sessions. In the case of hill intervals, you'll notice that as your fitness improves, not only will your heart rate be several beats lower at the end of every hill interval you perform but it will also drop that much quicker too. The increased size and strength of the heart means that clearing away unwanted metabolic by-products such as lactic acid is easier and the heart has an easier time to facilitate the process than it did months previously.

From these examples alone, you can see how keeping an e-diary or an old fashioned notebook to record this simple information is an invaluable part of your training. Seeing your physiological improvements week on week or month on month does wonders for your confidence and gives you peace of mind that you are training correctly and making fitness gains.

HEART RATE AND ILL HEALTH

There are instances, however, where you'll notice little wobbles during which the data doesn't seem to add up. Fluctuations in heart rate are common and can be warning signs that either your body is struggling to adapt to environmental changes or you are coming down with a virus.

Everyone has off days during training, which can happen for any number of reasons, from the wrong mindset to poor nutrition, or it can simply be just one of those days. However, for those times when an impending virus such as a cold has invaded you and is waiting in the wings to express itself, initial signs of the bug can often be picked up on your heart rate monitor.

In times of impending ill health, your resting and active heart rate often beats a good 5–10 beats faster than normal, so if you notice any of the following signs, be prepared to do battle with an unwelcome virus for the upcoming days:

- Elevated heart rate at rest
- Elevated heart rate during moderate exercise
- Difficulty in maintaining your usual pace, despite running in your usual steady pace zone

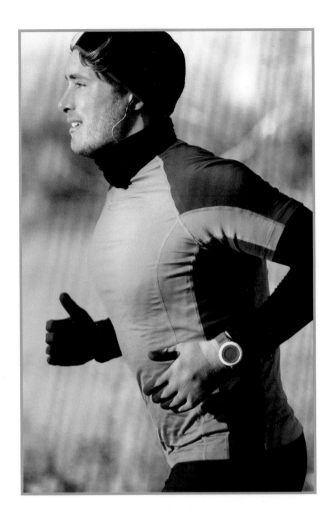

the ambient temperature shifts from cold windy weather to hot dry and/or humid conditions, our heart responds accordingly to keep the body functioning as efficiently as possible. Although more detail and advice is given about how to best prepare for training in extreme conditions in Chapter 9, it is worth pointing out a few key facts about how the heart specifically reacts to environmental conditions here.

RUNNING IN THE HEAT

Of all the weather conditions to be wary about, it is running in the heat. Trail runners should understand the level of heart rate variability they can expect when out on the trails during warm conditions. The body's core temperature warms up rapidly through a combination of the heat generated from the working muscles and the inescapable heat from the atmosphere. In a bid to cool down, the body responds by increasing the rate of sweating and pushing blood to the surface of the skin to help release heat. Both these factors cause the heart rate to rise and wreak havoc with your suggested heart rate training zones.

This situation is a perfect example of why heart rate training should be used as a guide rather than a rule. Although your heart rate might be several beats higher due to the ambient temperature, it doesn't necessarily mean that you need to slow down to settle back into your planned heart rate zone. If your body is tolerating the intensity of your run despite the heat and your training run isn't particularly long, this is the perfect time to be flexible with your heart rate zone.

However, the longer your planned training run in the heat, the more aware you should be of your heart rate. Although over time you will build up a tolerance of running in the heat, in the early stages of training, running long distances with an elevated heart rate due to the heat can lead to premature fatigue and

- It takes longer for your heart rate to return to resting rate
- Your legs feels heavy, weak and unresponsive

If a cold does express itself a few days after noticing these symptoms, don't try to fight it and soldier on despite feeling under the weather. Instead, take a few days off training and give your body the chance to fight off the virus.

ENVIRONMENTAL INFLUENCES ON HEART RATE

As well as human individuality, the environment we run in also has a massive effect on how our heart responds to exercise. As the seasons change and

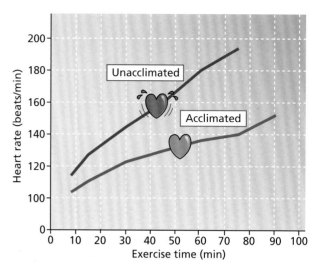

>> *Figure 5.2 Heart rate adaption from running in the heat*

dehydration – even if you are carrying fluid. Do not take the heat lightly in the early stages of training, particularly if you are not used to running in warm conditions. The effects of heat exhaustion can hit you in an instant and if you're off road and miles away from help, the trek home could be a long one.

As a general rule, allow a 5 per cent increase in heart rate above your usual level when running in the heat, but if it rises and remains 10 per cent higher than normal, slow down, cool down and think very carefully about continuing further. If in doubt, cut your run short and head home.

RUNNING IN THE COLD

From one extreme to another, running in cold weather has the opposite effect to that of running in the heat. Often, you may find your heart rate is 5–10 per cent lower than usual when running at the same pace, as the cold ambient temperature keeps your body temperature cool and your heart is not having to work quite so hard to prevent you from over-heating.

The main thing to consider when running in cold temperatures is to avoid the instinctive desire to put

>> *You risk a higher heart rate when running in the heat.*

>> *You risk a lower heart rate when running in the cold.*

on excessive clothing. Although initially it might feel like a wise move and you set off into the ice-cold air feeling snug in your two or three layers, as your time on the trail ticks by and you start to warm up, the sweat you begin to produce can actually end up leading to excessive heat loss. How? The more you sweat, the more chance it has of soaking through your layers leading to heat being removed through evaporation of the sweat. This has the ultimate consequence of encouraging your body to lose heat at a faster rate, leading to a situation all trail runners must avoid when running remote trails – a drop in body temperature.

LET YOUR HEAD RULE YOUR HEART

Remember, if something doesn't feel quite right and you feel unwell, dizzy or disoriented while out running, despite your heart functioning well within a 'steady run' heart rate zone, use your common sense – just because your heart is functioning well within its means it doesn't necessarily mean that other systems in your body are – so stop. Low blood sugar, or even low electrolyte levels can all make you feel ill without affecting your heart rate – so rather than running yourself into the ground on a remote trail instead stop, think and do the sensible thing and call someone.

The decision to use a heart rate monitor for training is a personal choice – I may be passionate about it, and hopefully I've made some persuasive arguments in this chapter – but if it's not for you don't go spending a fortune on a gadget you'll never use – save that for the travel expenses to your next race instead!

06

STRETCHING FOR THE TRAILS

Despite how much we now know about the importance of stretching both before and after training, it still surprises me how few runners stretch at all. Even more surprising is the alarmingly high percentage of runners I see stretching before running who actually stretch incorrectly and risk injuring themselves before they've even taken a single step.

Stretching is very much a science and getting that science right should be an integral part of your trail running training. A good stretching routine for all your key muscles both before a run and as part of your pre-hab during time off the trails will help to ensure your muscle fibres are elongated and are able to contract freely and without restriction. Neglecting to stretch can cause fibres to shorten and creates tension in your muscles, which in turn can lead to biomechanical imbalances, inflammation and ultimately injury.

MOBILITY BEFORE STRETCHING

As a trail runner joint mobility is something you should also take seriously – and it is the perfect preparation for stretching – especially for the early morning runners among us.

Joints are lubricated by synovial fluid, which helps to coat the articular cartilage (a waxy covering on the end of bones to help joints move smoothly) at the end of the bones. Mobility exercises help to encourage a good flow of synovial fluid to the joints, ensuring they can easily go through a full range of movement and make the stretches you go on to do far more effective.

Mobility exercises don't have to take long and are incredibly easy to perform. The two that follow are examples of mobility exercises ideally suited for trail runners. Do them at home before you head out the door or on the trail before your run.

EXERCISE 6.1 Ankle clocks

Due to the uneven terrain out on the trails, good mobility of the ankle joint is essential to help prevent injury. Simply put your ankle joints through the 12 points of an imaginary clock. Start off by dorsiflexing your ankle (lifting it upwards) then pointing to '12 o'clock'. Then raise the foot again and point it towards 1 o'clock, etc. Go around the clock and then finish doing a few full circular rotations of the ankle joint.

EXERCISE 6.2 Knee lifts

Alternating knee lifts are a great way to put your hip and knee joints through a good range of movement to get that synovial fluid flowing. From a standing position, lift your knee up to your chest then drop it down and extend your leg back as far as is comfortable. Bring the knee back up to the chest and repeat five times on each leg.

LOOK AFTER YOUR MUSCLES

Although your days as a road runner are in many ways similar to those spent on the trails, as far as your muscles are concerned, negotiating complex running surfaces peppered with tree roots, uneven ground and sudden changes in incline gives them a bit more of a hard time. The muscles of the lower leg go through an especially tough ride as the ankle joints and their associated muscles have to adapt very quickly to unexpected changes in the running surface. Although the speed at which the muscles have to react is more often than not well within the neuromuscular capabilities of the body, if the associated muscles are excessively tight and therefore constantly under excessive tension, tendon inflammation and injuries may very well be waiting around the corner for you.

KEY PLAYERS

If you were to ask a dozen physiotherapists what the most common causes of running injury are, the majority would probably put tight muscles at the top of the list. Many will want to find the root cause of the tightness to discover how it got so tight but, either way, a predominant part of rehabilitation will be to focus on stretching those tight muscles.

As a trail runner, although there are potentially dozens of muscles that require stretching to keep your body on the straight and narrow, there are several key players you'd be wise to stretch on a regular basis (see static stretching on p. 96)

BE STRETCH SPECIFIC

Knowing which muscles you should focus on is only half the story. There are actually several types of stretching for different occasions, and while it won't necessarily result in injury, choosing the wrong stretch at the wrong time may very well end up being a waste of time and defeat the object of stretching altogether.

STATIC STRETCHING

Static stretches are best done at home on your non-run days. Holding a muscle at the point of bind (stretch) for a prolonged period of time and gradually increasing the range of movement as the muscle fibres relax is a great pre-hab exercise to avoid injury. Static stretching is also ideal when you are recovering from injury as it helps to elongate the muscle fibres and make them far more efficient at contracting once you hit the trails again.

Static stretching is vital for any trail runner who feels they have tight muscles. Most of us are born with a certain number of tight muscles and although there is a chance they could lie dormant and not pose an injury risk, there is no harm in spending some time stretching them on a regular basis.

Many road and trail runners still use static stretching as part of a warm-up before a run, and although this is not harmful, static stretching alone before you are about to exercise doesn't do much to wake up your body and nervous system in preparation for hitting a hard run. This is where dynamic stretching comes in.

DYNAMIC STRETCHING

As the name implies, dynamic stretching involves movement. By stretching a muscle using **controlled** movements, you not only stretch the muscle fibres very effectively and under complete control, but you also stimulate the nervous system and increase blood flow to the muscles at the same time. This form of stretching, therefore, is the best way to prepare for the trails. If you prepare using static stretches alone, you'll begin your run with a low heart rate and relatively sluggish blood flow to all your key muscles – not ideal. Prepare for your run with dynamic stretches and you'll have significant blood flow to your muscles and a decent heart rate, which will allow you to effectively hit the ground running.

THE STRETCHES

Now you know why we stretch and you understand the suitability of one type of stretch over another, you're ready to learn how to perform them correctly and safely. The following stretches relate to the key muscles and are those I believe should be performed

THE LUCKY BENDY FEW

Contrary to popular belief, not everyone needs to stretch. Some people are born with more supple muscles than others and trying to stretch muscles, which do not need to be lengthened, can actually do more harm than good. As a general rule, if a muscle is tight then stretch it, if it's not then it is often best left alone.

This leads to the obvious question – how do you know if a muscle is tight or not? There is no easy answer and it is often best left to a physiotherapist to decide, but more often than not, you'll know if a muscle feels tight and needs some attention. For example, if you are in a standing position and perform a simple thigh stretch by grabbing hold of your foot behind your back and pulling it towards your backside, you'll soon know if you need to stretch. Some runners will be able to do this without any problems and without feeling any significant stretching sensation in the thigh, others may get halfway and struggle to pull it any further. I think it is obvious who needs to stretch here.

every time you take to the trails and administered statically to any excessively tight muscles during your rest and recovery periods. As you meet more experienced trail runners, you'll no doubt pick up on some other great stretches to incorporate into your routine.

Of course there are many more stretches for other muscles not mentioned here and if you feel pain or tightness in a particular muscle not included below, please seek professional advice.

STRETCHING TIPS

Although stretching is generally a very safe form of muscle preparation, care must still be taken to avoid placing muscles under excessive tension when performing a stretch. To make sure you stretch safely, here are a few tips:

- Work yourself slowly into the stretch and remember to only go to the point of bind, where you feel the initiation of the stretch. You'll know you've reached this point when you feel that the muscle begins to tighten and is reluctant to move any further through the range of movement.
- It's not a competition. If a training friend is able to put their leg through a greater range of movement than you, this isn't an invitation to compete and match their level of flexibility. We're all different.
- If a muscle is already flexible, do not stretch it further. There is no additional benefit and it could do more harm than good.
- It's best to make sure muscles are warm before you stretch, since they are far more pliable when warm. Jog a few hundred metres first or at the very least move around a bit to encourage blood flow to the muscles.

MAXIMISING DYNAMIC STRETCHES

Convenience and time (and lack thereof) are often the two biggest reasons why runners either neglect to stretch at all before a run or keep it as brief as possible. If these excuses sound familiar, try combining the dynamic exercises below into one fluid routine. Simply begin jogging, then perform one dynamic stretch for 10–15 seconds, then another and so on until you've performed each of the stretches. Turn around and repeat the process, this time incorporating a few different stretches.

By performing this routine several times, in five minutes you'll not only be well stretched but also incredibly warm and ready to run.

GLUTES

There are several significant glute muscles which could do with being stretched before and after training, making it tricky to find one overall stretch for the region. However, the static stretch on the next page is perhaps the most effective for targeting all major glute muscles.

EXERCISE 6.3 Static glute stretch

This is a great general stretch for your glutes (including the deep glute muscle, piriformis).

ACTION

- Kneel down on the floor of your living room or on a soft trail, resting your upper body on your forearms.

- Cross one knee over the other and slowly extend and straighten it backwards.

- As you straighten the leg, you'll notice that your bottom slowly moves back and you'll start to feel a lovely stretch in the glutes.

- Hold the stretch for 15–20 seconds then repeat with the opposite leg.

EXERCISE 6.4 Dynamic glute stretch

This is best performed at the start of your run on a flat, even surface.

ACTION

- Begin the stretch by deciding if you are going to stand on the spot or perform the stretch on the run – personally I find that performing it on the run is better.

- Simply drive one thigh upwards while at the same time pumping your opposing arm forwards.

- Perform this movement on every stride, alternating leg drive and arm drive.

- Start off gently, slowly building the speed and range of movement of the thigh driving upwards.

HAMSTRINGS

The hamstrings are one of the easiest muscles to stretch and of those runners who *do* stretch, they are perhaps the most commonly stretched of the muscles. In some cases of injury or dysfunction you may need to perform a more targeted stretch to focus on the parts of the hamstring muscle attaching to the knee or the pelvis, but as a general stretch the following is a good one.

EXERCISE 6.5 Static hamstring stretch

ACTION

- If at home, you can perform this stretch with a chair, table or couch on to which you place your foot. If you are on the trail, find some even ground or stand next to a fence, gate or wall if there is one. Some people like to place their foot on a raised platform – this is up to you.

- With the leg you want to stretch extended in front of you, bend the supporting leg slightly and, if required, rest your hand gently on your thigh if you find it more comfortable to do so or you need to bend lower to get deeper stretch.

- Very slowly, lean your upper body forward, ensuring your back remains straight. After leaning 20 or so degrees you will feel a stretching sensation on the back of the extended leg.

- Hold the stretch for 15–20 seconds (or until you feel the stretch), then repeat with the other leg.

EXERCISE 6.6 Dynamic hamstring stretch – standing still

ACTION

- Like the dynamic glute stretch, this can be performed standing still or on the run.

- If standing still, simply slowly swing your leg forwards and backwards, always under complete control.

- Gradually increase the range of movement as you feel the tension in the hamstrings begin to ease.

- Perform this pendulum-like swing for 30 seconds.

EXERCISE 6.7 Dynamic hamstring stretch – on the run

ACTION

- Find a smooth trail surface without any significant ridges or potential ankle twisting hazards.

- In a skipping motion, extend and swing one leg out in front of you and return it to the ground.

- Perform a skipping motion as you change legs, then extend and swing the other leg forward.

- Perform this for 20m or so, turn around, then come back, performing the same stretch

CALVES

Arguably the hardest worked muscles during running, you need to look after your calves before, during and after training. Due to the work they put in on the trails, the calf muscles have a tendency to tighten up quite easily and it's vital you stretch them regularly to keep the fibres elongated and contracting smoothly.

EXERCISE 6.8 Static calf stretch

ACTION

- Find a solid tree or wall on which to place your hands.

- With your front leg bent, extend the other leg well behind you, keeping your heel placed on the ground.

- Slowly lean forwards, keeping your rear heel on the ground and your back leg straight. You should start to feel quite an intense stretch on the calf muscle of this back leg.

- Hold the stretch for 15–20 seconds then repeat with the other leg.

- You can change the emphasis of the stretch by bringing the back leg in a foot or so and bending the leg at the knee – but remember to keep your heel on the ground.

EXERCISE 6.9 Dynamic calf stretch

This can be performed in exactly the same position as the static calf stretch, the only difference being that you integrate movement into the stretch.

ACTION

- Assume the same position as for the static stretch, the only difference being that you extend both legs back, with a slight bend at the knee.

- Then while bending the knee, raise the heel of one foot off the floor and move it back to the ground to initiate a stretch.

- Simply alternate this movement between both legs, gradually increasing the speed.

- As a general rule, the further back you position your legs, the greater the stretch.

QUADRICEPS

Like the hamstrings, the quadriceps (thighs/quads) are another easily stretched muscle and quad stretches can be performed at any time and place.

If you find your quads are often tight after training runs, try to stretch them as often as you can. Half a dozen times a day is certainly not excessive if you feel you are tight in this area.

EXERCISE 6.10 Static quadriceps stretch

ACTION

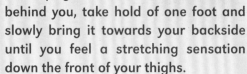

- Find an even trail with or without something close by to hold on to. If you are at home, you can adapt the stretch to lying face down on the floor.

- Standing (or lying face down) nice and upright, reach behind you, take hold of one foot and slowly bring it towards your backside until you feel a stretching sensation down the front of your thighs.

- As some of you may be more flexible than others, it's perfectly possible your foot could reach your backside without feeling any stretch. If this is the case, you can increase the stretch by slowly tilting the bottom of your pelvis upwards, increasing the pull on your quads.

- Hold the stretch for 10–15 seconds, then repeat with the other leg. Feel free to repeat the process two or three times, or until your quads feel stretched.

EXERCISE 6.11 Dynamic quadriceps stretch

This can be performed in exactly the same position as the static calf stretch, the only difference being that you integrate movement into the stretch.

ACTION

- Assume the same position as for the static stretch, but this time extend both legs back, with a slight bend at the knee.

- Then while bending the knee, raise the heel of one foot off the floor and move it back to the ground to initiate a stretch.

- Simply alternate this movement between both legs, gradually increasing the speed.

- As a general rule, the further back you position your legs, the greater the stretch.

ADDUCTORS (GROIN)

Many runners tend to neglect the inside leg muscles, yet the importance of stretching the adductors before a trail run should not be underestimated.

The adductors serve as a great stabiliser during the running gait and are worked particularly hard when you take on inclines. If you have a hilly session ahead, make sure the following stretches are done well.

EXERCISE 6.12 Static adductor stretch

ACTION

- Find a smooth trail surface, preferably not gravel – slipping during this stretch could cause an eye-watering injury! If you are performing the stretch at home, a carpeted surface is ideal.

- Face forwards and extend one leg to the side with your foot angled 45 degrees away from you. The other leg must remain straight with the foot pointing forwards.

- Slowly shift your weight to the side of the bent leg and you will begin to feel a stretch on the inside of the straight leg.

- Make sure your hips are facing forwards at all times or you won't feel the maximum benefit of the stretch.

- Hold the stretch for 15–20 seconds, then repeat with the other leg.

EXERCISE 6.13 Dynamic adductor stretch

ACTION

- Although this stretch can be done without holding on to anything, it's often easier if you perform this stretch holding on to a tree or wall.

- Facing forwards, slowly begin to swing one leg (keeping it straight) across your body, as if you were kicking a football with the inside of your foot.

- In a pendulum motion, swing your leg a little further away from the body with every swing so that you are kicking the imaginary football a little harder with each swing.

- This stretch has the added benefit of stretching certain glute muscles during the phase of swing where your leg comes across the body.

- Perform this swinging movement for 30 seconds and then change legs.

HIP FLEXORS

Arguably the most complex group of muscles in a runner's body, the hip flexors are key players in the health of your back, knees and general running ability. Many injuries often originate from tight hip flexors, so look after them and always make sure you stretch them well before and after training.

EXERCISE 6.14 Static hip flexor stretch

ACTION

- Kneel down on the floor or on a soft verge and extend one leg in front of you, bent at 90 degrees from the hip and 90 degrees from the knee.

- From this position, slowly rotate your pelvis upwards. Imagine your pelvis is a bucket full of water and you're tipping a little bit of water out over your backside.

- The rotation of the pelvis alone might initiate a stretching sensation down the front of your rear leg but if it doesn't, slowly move your whole body forwards until you feel a stretch.

- Hold the stretch for 15–20 seconds, then repeat on the other leg.

- You can perform an alternative, and slightly more effective stretch if you assume a similar position but in a standing lunge position with your back leg slightly bent (this alternative is ideal if the ground is either dry and hard or wet or boggy).

EXERCISE 6.15 Dynamic hip flexor stretch

You'll get a good hip flexor stretch when you perform the 'standing still' dynamic hamstring stretch. When your leg swings to the back (extension), you may feel a nice stretch on your hip flexor muscles at the top of your thighs. As an alternative, you could try the following stretch.

ACTION

- Assume the same position as the static hip flexor stretch, but reduce the amount of pelvic rotation a little if you tilted it to get that extra stretch.

- Starting off slowly and gently, move your body into the stretch by moving forwards and backwards.

- Gradually increase your range of movement.

- This stretch can also be performed in the standing lunge position as explained above.

- Perform for 20–30 seconds on each leg.

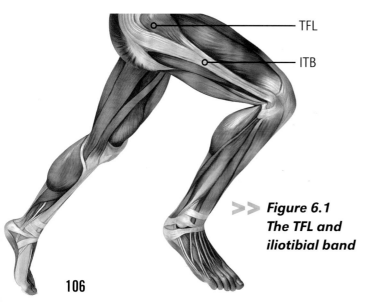

— TFL

— ITB

>> *Figure 6.1*
The TFL and
iliotibial band

ILIOTIBIAL BAND (ITB)

The iliotibial band (ITB) is a long fibrous band running down the outside of the leg, which inserts just on the outside of the knee joint. Through training and a lack of attention to stretching, this band can become very tight and cause inflammation either near the hip joint or the knee joint, leading to a significant amount of pain and an enforced rest from running for several weeks. This condition, known as ITB syndrome, is very common in runners and although wearing the wrong running shoes and over-zealous training practices can cause it, you can avoid and manage it through regular stretching.

The problem with stretching the ITB is that it is very awkward and often a conventional stretch is ineffective. To effectively prevent ITB syndrome what you should actually be trying to do is stretch the muscle that runs from the pelvis along the outer thigh, known as the tensor fascia latae (TFL). The ITB attaches to the TFL, so stretching both releases tension and stops an inflammatory response at the knee or hip.

Although there are other stretches available, by far the most effective treatment for these structures is **foam rolling** or, more scientifically, **self-myofascial release**. You can purchase foam rollers anywhere online by simply entering the term into a search engine; they are a widely and cheaply available piece of equipment that should really be an integral part of any trail runner's kit.

EXERCISE 6.16 Self-myofascial release

Self-myofascial release is a highly effective form of treatment to encourage the body to let go of muscular tension within muscle and fascia. In the case of a tight ITB, you will find that by applying pressure to its tender spots and staying on the tender spot for 30 seconds or so, it will gradually ease and become a lot less tender. The release of this tension all along the ITB helps to relax and loosen it, thus helping towards preventing injury further down the line.

Although many sports massage therapists perform a similar form of release on the ITB and other structures, with the help of the foam roller you can do something similar at home.

ACTION
- Lie down on your side as shown in top picture
- Start at the top of the ITB, at the top and side of your leg. As a rough guide, you should start the roll in the same place where your pocket would be if you were wearing trousers

- When you hit a tender spot (you'll know it when you do!), stop and stay on it for around 30–45 seconds
- Don't let the pain become greater than 7/10 (0 = no pain and 10 = excruciating). If the pain is too great, you'll want to tense up, therefore making the release of the tension in the tendon ineffective.
- When the tenderness subsides, move down until you find the next tender spot.
- Go all the way to the lateral side (outside) of the knee, then repeat on the other leg.

07

TRAINING FOR THE TRAILS

When you picked up this book, it may have come as a bit of a surprise that it would take until Chapter 7 to start talking about how to go about getting you fit for the trails. You can clock up as many miles as you like, but without a strong core, knowledge about how to negotiate trail paths, how to kit yourself out for the trails and what effect trail running has on the body, there's a good chance your enjoyment of trail running could be short lived.

TRAINING FOR YOU

Our genetic make-up has a huge influence over which aspects of running we will excel at, so to apply a rule of thumb to a group of new trail runners is next to useless. Some runners are like mountain goats and can run uphill all day long, yet struggle to maintain a fast-tempo pace on the flat, while others are able to hold high speeds on the flat, yet are gasping for breath after a series of small inclines.

At the end of the day, you are what you are and although you can work on your weaknesses to become a better runner and competitor, it is important to understand that you have to train in tune with your body and no one else's. No matter what you read on forums or Google searches,

the opinions and advice of other (well-meaning) runners should be taken with caution and not seen as a definitive answer to your running or training questions. Accept you'll make mistakes, but learn from them and they'll make you a stronger and far more capable runner.

For all the complexities and contradictions surrounding the subject of training, there are several key principles that even the most argumentative of trail running disciples would find it difficult to argue against.

BASE TRAINING

It might be a little presumptuous, but there's a good chance your interest in trail running and desire to embrace it has evolved from many years as a road runner. If this is the case, the good news is that over the years of pounding the pavements, you have built up a very good level of base fitness and you're unlikely to have any problems traversing a trail route for an hour or so. Just how competently, balanced and graciously you could execute such a run is of course a different matter, but there's a good chance your heart and lungs will have no problems meeting the fitness requirements necessary to see you over the trail.

If you are completely new to running however, and have decided to hit the trails as your first form of running, then take your time to gradually build

>> *Clocking up the trail hours*

up your fitness. The views you get from the trails make it arguably a better place to take up running, so enjoy your surroundings and increase your time on the trails slowly.

Even if you have got previous experience, does this mean you are ready to tackle the more challenging forms of training, such as intervals on trail hills, to get you into awesome trail-running shape? Not at all – your apprenticeship has only just begun.

BUILDING AN AEROBIC BASE

Long-distance running and your ability to do it well, without undue fatigue and for a long period of time, is predominantly down to how well your aerobic system is conditioned. When used in conjunction with fat and carbohydrate stores, oxygen is your key fuelling ingredient since it ultimately powers the muscles during your low intensity steady runs.

Although you may be well aware of the aerobic system from your experience as a road runner, you need to build on it before hitting the challenging trails.

THE TRAIL RUNNER'S AEROBIC SYSTEM

As a general guide, your aerobic zone or capacity lies in or around 65–80 per cent of your maximum heart rate, or a level of intensity where you are able to exercise while still holding a conversation. When road running, this intensity is fairly easy to maintain as conditions underfoot are consistent, and even when faced with a hill, it's simple to ease off the pace a little and stay pretty much within the limits of your aerobic capacity. When trail running, however, you have far less control over your ability to stay in your aerobic zone, primarily due to the nature of the terrain. Undulating trail paths impact the stabilising muscles of the core and lower leg, forcing them and, therefore, your aerobic system, to work much harder. Unlike road running where these sudden increases in muscle recruitment are few and far between, they happen all the time on the trail.

WHAT IS A STEADY PACE?

The term steady pace has often come under fire from the running community, mostly because of its ambiguity. Does it mean steady as in fast steady or slow steady, or somewhere in between? Naturally, Google the term and in some running forum somewhere there'll be someone claiming to own its true meaning, but in my opinion you can translate the word steady in any way you like.

In the early stages of your trail-running adventures, a steady run is more likely to mean a pace that is fairly slow and one of which you are very much in control. It should feel comfortable; you should be able to sustain it for a good hour or two without fearing you'll collapse in a heap.

As your trail fitness improves, however, and your tolerance of the terrain develops, a steady run might be performed at a reasonable pace that makes conversation a struggle. Some runners see it as a pace which is a few notches below that of a tempo run (*see* page 120).

On the basis some runners are physiologically better equipped to maintain higher running speeds than others, my view is that a steady run is an individual interpretation and varies from one runner – and one trail path – to another. Ultimately, don't let semantics define your training – you'll be a far better trail runner if you define running terminology in tandem with your own ability and training goals.

>> *Varied terrain makes running tougher.*

When you're not used to it, the subtle demands for more energy as you leap over a stream, climb over a rock or negotiate a muddy trail, can take their toll and you will tire much more quickly as your running effort increases to more than 80 per cent of your maximum heart rate. Put simply, you leave your aerobic zone and push into your anaerobic zone. While that's not a problem once in a while, it is tiring and energy sapping over the course of a one-hour trail run. Therefore, in the early stages of your trail-running career you'll experience greater variability within your aerobic zone as your body tries to adapt to the demands of the trails. Although you might consider yourself to be in good enough shape to easily tolerate an hour-long steady run on the road, try to keep your expectations in check when you are testing out your aerobic fitness on the trail.

IMPROVING YOUR AEROBIC ZONE

Improving your aerobic capacity on the trails is essentially no different to on the road. Regular steady, or even easy training runs on progressively more challenging and demanding trail routes gradually builds your tolerance and teaches your muscles to learn how to tolerate sudden changes of intensity. However, keep in mind the duration, condition and topography of the trail race for which you are training.

BE SPECIFIC

If you don't have a specific trail race in mind and you are simply trail running for the fun of it, by all means feel free to play around on as many different trail routes as you like to build your aerobic fitness. Even if you are training for a race, there is equally no reason why you can't train on a variety of different trail routes in the early stages of training. However, in the months leading up to race day, it's essential you make your training a little more specific.

The secret to successful race preparation is to have an in-depth knowledge of the race route. By adopting the principles of the 'Five Ps' (Prior Planning Prevents Poor Performance), you can ensure no stone is left unturned and be confident that you are race fit and race ready.

So, with this in mind, when you begin to turn your attention to race-specific training, acquire as much information about your race as possible. This should include:

- **Inclines:** What is their gradient? How regular are they? Where do they occur?
- **Conditions underfoot:** Will the trail be muddy, wet, complex, rocky?
- **Weather:** What conditions can you expect or were experienced in previous years – hot, cold, wet, windy?
- **Duration:** How far is the race? How long do you expect to be running for?

All these factors should play a big part in how you prepare for your race. By basing your aerobic training runs on the predicted/expected race conditions, you are training your body in a highly specific manner to tolerate the trail and keep you well within your aerobic zone. If you spend weeks or months training

DO WHAT YOU CAN

As easy as it is to tell you to make your training as specific as you can, in practice this is not always possible. Training for a winter race on a hilly (and likely wet) course is not easy or practical if you live miles away from hilly trail routes and Mother Nature doesn't give you the rain to muddy up those trails in time for your practice. So, just do what you can. Factor in as many of the race day variables as you can and include the others when possible.

on flat, dry and un-complex trails, you're going to get one heck of a shock come race day if the route is hilly, soggy and complex. You can be as conditioned as you like on the trails you've been training on, but your race day will likely leave you exhausted and with memories you'd rather forget.

TOP TIPS FOR IMPROVING YOUR AEROBIC FITNESS

- Perform at least one or two long, slow runs a week, with one of them longer than the other.
- Increase the distance of your long, slow run by no more than 10–15 per cent per week.
- Vary the trail surface every now and again to condition the body to tolerate surface variations.
- Practise wearing your back pack/hydration pack during your aerobic training sessions.
- Always tell someone where you are going and plan your route beforehand.
- Running with someone else is both safer and a lot more fun.

HILL TRAINING

If you don't like hills, I'd strongly reconsider whether trail running is for you! That's not to say that all trail routes are peppered with inclines, but due to the type of landscape trail routes occur on, inclines will feature fairly regularly throughout your training.

Regardless of how mountainous your anticipated race, integrating hills into your training plan will boost your trail running fitness to new heights. Long duration or repetitive incline training places huge demands on your legs and cardiovascular system, thus encouraging the body to adapt to the additional stresses. The lung- and leg-burn might not initially be your idea of fun, but when you see what a difference hill sessions make to your running ability, you'll find the pain gets curiously addictive.

No matter where you live or what sort of trails you're going to be training on, there is a good chance there'll be a number of hilly trails nearby.

>> *Tackling inclines*

But when you first start out trail running, my advice is to avoid tackling extreme hills or undertaking high-intensity hill training sessions for at least the first few weeks. Although many naively think that running is running, taking on steep inclines on a trail is a very different proposition to hill reps on the road, so before you hit these sessions hard, spend a few weeks getting used to the conditions underfoot and learn from every run. Once you have gained some experience on several different trail routes, then it's time to go and find some hills and have some seriously good lung-busting fun.

Before you take on those hills, it's worth taking a look at your uphill running technique. Technique has far more importance to hill running than many runners give it credit, so help to maximise your efficiency by changing your technique.

UPHILL RUNNING TECHNIQUE

Running uphill for long distances often puts the fear of God into new trail runners. The sensation of burning thighs, a thumping heart and relentless inclines can make the experience fairly gruelling and uncomfortable and one that can take a while to get used to.

There continues to be much speculation as to whether your uphill running technique has much of an effect on your performance and, if so, whether there are certain tricks that can make those long, steady climbs any more bearable. The answer is both yes and no.

Ultimately, without a solid base of aerobic (and anaerobic) fitness you are always going to struggle on the hills. Without a good capillary network helping to provide the legs with oxygen and removing the waste products after muscle contraction, your legs are going to pack up in the very early stages of a hill

run. Irrespective of technique, a good level of fitness is vital if you are to master the hills.

Once you have developed that fitness, or even while you are in the process of developing it, these following uphill running techniques will help you to climb the hills with maximum efficiency and even grace.

TIP 1: RELAX

Tensing up when running on the flat is common enough, but tensing up when tackling hills is incredibly common. When you tense up, you significantly reduce your running efficiency as a proportion of blood is diverted away from the legs and used to contract peripheral tense muscles such as the musculature around the shoulders. Make a conscious effort to relax your shoulders and approach the inclines with a relaxed frame of mind. You'll be surprised how much easier the climb will then become.

TIP 2: SLOW IT DOWN

There is no shame in dropping your pace when running up a hill. Walking on particularly steep hills is perfectly normal in many hilly trail races, so do not try to be superhuman and conquer the hill at speed. Drop your pace and take the intensity out of the incline.

TIP 3: DEVELOP A RHYTHM

Running at a constant rhythm is incredibly useful on the hills. A good rhythm helps control your breathing and assists in an economy of effort. Many seasoned trail runners use a small-stride rhythm, particularly when the gradient increases. Stick to a rhythm and you'll find your comfort levels increase dramatically.

TIP 4: FOREFOOT STRIKE

The steeper the incline, the more beneficial you'll find forefoot striking when it comes to body position.

>> Focus is also important when running on the trails

By striking the ground with the forefoot first you are automatically shifting your body weight, and centre of gravity, slightly forwards, thereby giving you momentum for your next stride. This has the ultimate effect of increasing your running efficiency.

TIP 5: USE YOUR ARMS

The arms are often under-used when hill running, yet their assistance during tough inclines can be hugely beneficial. We all know that sprinters use their arms to great effect to power themselves forwards, so adopting the same principle when attacking hills on a trail route can help to take a little bit of the intensity away from the legs. When the going gets tough, drive your arms forward as you run up the hill – it will still be tiring, but at least you'll give your overworked legs a bit of a respite.

TIP 6: LOOK UP

When you're trying to tackle a steep incline, it feels instinctive to look down at the trail in front of you rather than keep your head up and your eyes looking forward. Physiologically, the latter is far better for you. By keeping your head up and eyes looking forward, you keep the chest cavity wide open and allow the maximum amount of oxygen to be inhaled and used. Looking down has the opposite effect and can actually restrict your natural breathing pattern. So, embrace your surroundings and keep looking forwards – even if it is a long way to the top.

There are numerous types of hill training sessions, many of which you can integrate into your usual long runs (see page 119). Like your aerobic training sessions, always remember to keep your training as specific as possible to your anticipated race the closer it gets.

LONG, SLOW HILLS

Training on trail routes featuring a generous selection of steady inclines helps to condition your legs, muscles and cardiovascular system. By performing these runs at a steady pace and within your aerobic training zone, you will improve your aerobic efficiency – the by-product of which is to help the muscles operate efficiently and without undue stress.

Most long trail routes feature their fair share of inclines at some point or another, so you may not have to go out of your way to train on such routes. However, it is here that the issue of specificity comes into play. For example, if your upcoming race has one, long, drawn out 1000ft climb after 5 miles, or several short but steep climbs scattered along the course, you'll have to slowly begin to work it into your training sessions. If you don't have a 1000ft hill anywhere near you to practise on, then training on a 200ft climb five times (at least) is the best way forward.

As your competence and fitness gets better in the coming months, aim to improve not only the length of time you spend on hilly routes, but try to train on routes featuring more challenging inclines. The extra work they demand of your heart and lungs prevents your fitness from plateauing and will ultimately make you an even more efficient runner.

TOP TIPS FOR LONG, SLOW HILLS

- Start conservatively and build up the duration of your run over time.
- Run on trails with hills at different stages of your run – hills at the end of a run are great for both your physical and mental preparation.
- Don't be afraid to drop your pace a little on long, steep hills.

- Train on a variety of different surfaces. Muddy, rocky and dry trail routes all place different demands on your leg muscles.

WHAT GOES UP MUST COME DOWN

Once you have accepted that significant parts of your training will involve going uphill, you'll have to accept and master coming back down! Although fell runners take downhill running to the extreme (in 1910, it is believed a man called Ernest Dalzell ran the best part of a mile down an extreme slope in the Burnsall race, North Yorkshire at an average pace of 21mph, or 10.65 seconds/100m), the skill of running downhill at pace, as well as safely, is one which takes practice.

The general advice for anyone new to trail running is to first experiment with running down

by everyone who has trained themselves to handle the downslopes!

Over the course of a two- or three-hour trail race, the time you could save by running as opposed to carefully walking downhill is massive and when you consider that just a bit of practice will give you the competence to run instead of walk. It's time to get training. The sensation of hurtling down a trail slope in complete control and with confidence that you won't fall is exhilarating, but you'll need to develop this ability.

small slopes on a variety of different surfaces. Your feet, leg muscles and general ability to maintain your centre of gravity will all vary depending on what surface you are running on, so it's best to have a play on small hills at first to build up confidence.

SLIPPERY SLOPE

Trail surfaces, such as moveable scree (broken pieces of rock), slippery mud, shale and hard tracks, all offer you something different underfoot when trying to negotiate them at pace and with gravity on your back. Many runners new to the trails find it difficult to understand why seasoned runners place so much emphasis on running down hill – surely, if in doubt, you take it nice and slow? Well sure – if you want to be overtaken in a race

TOP TIPS FOR IMPROVING YOUR RUNNING DOWNHILL

Trail running may well have a good reputation for placing less stress on the joints than road running because of the running surface itself, but when it comes to running downhill, this perk can count for nothing. Hundreds of runners every year pick up a range of injuries from running downhill and although they are usually nothing more serious than a twisted ankle, it can make the trek home an incredibly long one. Lack of control, unfamiliarity with the surface, excessive speed and hidden rocks and roots are all possible reasons why you could find yourself in trouble on a downslope, so try these tips for improving the safety of your downhill running.

- Always wear trail shoes for downhill running – the extra grip is essential.
- Move your feet quickly. Practise spending as little time on each foot as possible.
- Don't be afraid to use your arms to help keep you balanced.
- Lean forwards for short downslopes and backwards for longer ones.
- Pick a spot a few feet in front of you so you know what's coming up next.
- Practise downhill running on a variety of long and short, steep slopes.

HILL INTERVALS

Many runners dread hill intervals or hill repeats. Lung-busting and thigh-burning sessions lasting sometimes for over an hour are incredibly demanding, but the fitness gains to be made from them are second to none.

DOWNHILL ETIQUETTE

Depending on your level of ability and courage, there is every chance that in a race situation, you'll be hurtling down hill way faster than someone else. If you are tearing down a slope and you notice you are gaining fast on a fellow runner, it's important you let them know of your presence to avoid a potentially nasty collision. As you get close to the slower runner and are within earshot, observe the trail ahead and choose which route you'll take as you pass. Then call out to the runner 'Passing on your left!' or 'Passing on your right!' to alert them to your presence.

NOTE: BEFORE YOUR HILL SESSION

Before you undertake any high-intensity hill session you must ensure you have warmed up well and run for at least 10–15 minutes before your first interval. Hill intervals are hard work and the extra strain they place on the muscles and tendons increases your risk of injury if you are not well warmed up and stretched (*see* Chapter 6 for suggested stretches).

Performing hill repeats on steep inclines is an incredibly good method of building leg strength and increasing your tolerance of hills on long training runs. By putting the body through challenging, high-resistance hill training sessions the body adapts by becoming more efficient at removing metabolic waste products from the leg muscles, thus helping you to keep running without undue fatigue and an excessively high heart rate.

There are of course several different types of hill interval sessions you can undertake, but the following are perhaps the most popular and beneficial to the majority of trail runners.

SHORT AND SHARP

These sessions are excellent at building your leg strength. Find a moderate to very steep hill. Ideally, the trail surface should be one which you are familiar with and/or similar to the type of trail on which you anticipate racing.

When you first attempt short and sharp hill sessions it is always best to err on the side of caution and go steady early on. Perform slightly fewer reps and if anything, undercook your pace. You can always go harder and faster in subsequent sessions, but these intervals are very demanding on

the body and should be treated with caution in the early days.

Session 1
- Perform 10–15 x 45–60-second fast-paced intervals up the hill.
- Walk down the slope then repeat.
- Look to build the repetitions up to 20 and or include a set of 10–15 press-ups at the bottom of the hill before you begin the next interval.

Session 2
- Perform 10–15 x 45–60-second fast-paced intervals up the hill.
- Halfway up, stop and perform 10 jump squats, then carry on to the top.
- Walk down the slope then repeat.

SHORT AND STEADY

Short and steady hill sessions are great for building both your cardiovascular fitness as well as your leg strength. Find a long moderate-to-steep hill, again with a trail surface you are familiar with. The tricky part about these sessions is finding a hill long enough, but as is often the case with trail running, seek and you will find (or double up on shorter trails).

Session 1
- Perform 6–8 x 5-minute steady runs up the hill.
- Jog (don't walk) down and repeat.
- Aim to increase this to 10–12 intervals.

Session 2
- Perform 8–10 x 4-minute intervals up the hill.
- Alternate your speed with a medium-fast and then a slow pace every minute.
- Walk down the slope and repeat.
- Aim to increase this to either more intervals or jog down the hill to reduce recovery time.

> **SURE FOOTED**
>
> As beneficial as hill training is for your trail running fitness, it will count for nothing if you get too confident on the trail slopes and end up tripping over a root or rock on fast ascent or descent.

>> *Get a grip*

TEMPO TRAINING

If you've spent years road running, you'll be all too familiar with the importance of tempo or threshold training. Running at a pace faster than steady and one which is hard, but possible, to sustain for medium-distance training runs provides an excellent starter session to help build up your tolerance to the accumulation of lactic acid. These sessions should ideally be performed once or twice a week and run on a variety of different trail routes ranging from hilly, to flat, to complex.

If you are using a heart rate monitor, your heart rate should be settling somewhere around the 80–90 per cent mark (depending on your level of fitness) and remain within that range for the majority of the run.

BASIC THRESHOLD SESSIONS

At first, when you are still getting used to the joys of trail running, your tempo sessions should be lasting somewhere in the region of 20–30 minutes. Although your tempo sessions may very well have lasted nearer to 45–60 minutes or more on the road, you must take the nature of the terrain into account and factor in that soft conditions underfoot may make the going that much tougher. So, with this in mind, have a play with your tempo sessions at first and see how you get on with them on the trails. Your running speed might not be massively quicker than that of your long slow runs,

but it still requires skill and practice to negotiate trail paths efficiently and safely while running at a fairly swift pace.

In summary, your basic tempo sessions in the early stages of training should be based around the following session:

- Find a trail route which is undulating, but not excessively hilly.
- Aim to spend at least 20–30 minutes on it, running at a pace which is too fast for you to be able to talk easily yet not so fast you build up high levels of lactic acid and are therefore unable to maintain your pace.

ADVANCED TEMPO SESSIONS

Once your confidence in both your threshold fitness and trail running competence grows, it's time to press on with further developing your threshold fitness. By increasing the distance and time you spend running at a threshold pace, your body will continue to adapt to the rigours of high intensity and sustained running, making you far more tolerant to running at high speeds without tiring. Prolonged tempo sessions are taxing on every muscle in your body, not least your calves, quadriceps and also your cardiovascular system, so be prepared to feel well and truly worked after a hard threshold run.

There are a number of ways you can advance your tempo sessions and there is no reason to make them the same every time. Provided you make them hard work, yet sustainable for a total of at least 60 minutes, you will be adding incredible value to your fitness. Have a play with the following threshold sessions and adapt them as you find necessary to the trail route you run them on.

Advanced tempo session 1

- Find a long trail route and spend the first 10–15 minutes jogging to warm up.
- After warming up, increase your pace to 85–90 per cent of your maximum pace (around 85–90 per cent of your maximum heart rate). You should find this pace taxing yet sustainable.
- Run at this pace on the trail for 45–60 minutes, aiming to maintain the same pace throughout.
- If you begin to tire before the session has finished you have gone off too fast and will need to slow down a notch or two next time.
- Over time, find a more challenging trail route by ensuring it features more incline or is more complex underfoot.

Advanced tempo session 2

- Head out for a run on your usual and familiar trail route and run at a steady pace for at least 10–15 minutes to warm up.
- After 15 minutes, run for 5 minutes at a speed which is a fraction faster than your tempo pace. As a rough guide, this is a few seconds per mile quicker than your 10k PB.

- After 5 minutes, rest for 1 minute and then repeat the whole sequence 6–8 times.
- To make this session harder, increase the time of intervals from 5 minutes, 10 or 15 minutes – increasing your rest time to 2 and 3 minutes respectively (ratio of 5:1).
- These are tough sessions but incredibly effective at boosting your fitness.

PROGRESSION IS KEY

There are no set rules for threshold training other than you should perform them at least once a week if you are training for a race, and that session should ultimately last anywhere from 45–60 minutes. However you choose to perform your threshold sessions, always remember that progression is the key to your continued fitness development. Staying on the same trail and running at the same pace for the same length of time session after session will lead to a plateau and prevent you from increasing your running fitness and trail competence. So when it comes to playing around with your threshold sessions, ask yourself whether you are making them progressively more challenging. Make a point of changing your threshold sessions every couple of weeks, even if it's a minor change. Remember: finishing the session you set out to do is essential – if you tire before the end, you have gone out too hard.

You can make the following tweaks one at a time or even all at once, if you're feeling brave:

- Reduce your recovery time between threshold intervals.
- Incorporate more inclines.
- Find a more taxing and complicated trail route.
- Increase the distance of your threshold session.

INTERVALS AND FARTLEK SESSIONS

Fartlek and interval sessions are the fastest paced sessions you'll perform in your training. Once again,

just because you are now a trail runner and spending time running off road, the terms 'interval' and 'fartlek' aren't really any different than their definition on the road. Short and sharp, high-speed intervals with little recovery are phenomenally good anaerobic training sessions that help you to develop an excellent tolerance to lactic acid and ultimately the ability to run at a faster pace for longer periods of time.

If you are serious about your trail running, high-intensity training drills are going to have to feature in your training regime at least once a week and on a variety of different surfaces.

WHICH IS BETTER?

Whether to go interval or fartlek can be confusing to those new to running, and the turmoil over which discipline to choose to help improve performance has caused much strife in my inbox over the years. As with most training theories, there are several schools of thought on which form of interval drill is better, but in my opinion it very much down to choice and what your specific goals are.

The key difference between interval and fartlek sessions is the structure.

INTERVALS

Intervals tend to be far more structured. From the outset you know you will be performing a set number of high-intensity intervals, for a set period of time or distance, with a set amount of rest between sets.

Interval sessions can take place anywhere and you do not necessarily need to perform them on the trails. Although you would ideally perform them on the same surface you plan to race on, performing them on an un-complex/smooth trail or the road might be easier and safer for some runners.

A typical example of an interval session might take place on a 45–60-minute (hazard-free) trail route and involve the following routine:

- Gentle jog for 5–10 minutes, then stretch.
- Run at 85–95 per cent of maximum pace for 2 minutes.
- Walk or jog gently for 3 minutes.
- Repeat cycle 8–10 times.

You can vary this session as much as you like and make it increasingly more difficult by running at pace for longer and/or reducing your recovery time. Provided you keep these sessions consistent and stick religiously to the timings of your active interval and rest period, you'll be able to compare one session to the next and chart improvement (this is where a training diary and/or heart rate monitor really comes into play – *see* chapter 5).

FARTLEK

Fartlek sessions are far less structured than interval sessions. A typical fartlek session involves you heading out for a 45–60-minute run and throwing in a series of high speed, varied distance intervals every now and again. Running on trails, there are a plethora of ways you can play around with fartlek sessions, for example:

- Significantly increase your pace every time you encounter a hill.
- Run hard for 2 minutes every time you see a felled tree/tree stump/stream.
- Run hard from one significant landmark to another.
- Run hard for 2–3 minutes every time your heart rate drops to a certain level.

The possibilities are endless, but the question you have to answer is which discipline is going to you suit you the best?

WHAT MAKES YOU TICK?

If, like me, you are a stickler for charting progress and religiously download your heart rate data after every training run and regularly compare previous training sessions, interval sessions will suit you best. The structured format of intervals makes it far easier to accurately compare one session against another; giving you all the information (and confidence) you need to confirm you are getting fitter and better tolerating the training. This is particularly important if you are training for an event rather than simply for fun and general fitness.

If, however, you are the type of person who is pretty chilled out about training and you're happy to gauge your improvements purely on how you feel during and after training runs, fartlek might be your preferred option. Provided you are true to yourself and promise to put in at least 10 hard efforts during the session, fartlek training can be fun without the pressure of looking at the clock every few minutes, waiting for your next high intensity interval.

ANAEROBIC SEMANTICS

At the end of the day, **effort**, **regularity** and **progression** are the three factors you need to ensure you are consistent in whatever form of high intensity/anaerobic training you do – be it structured intervals or instinctive fartlek. As a trail runner, the importance of hitting specific times for set intervals is far less important than it is to a road runner, so keep that in mind when planning your next high intensity training run.

Anaerobic training, such as advanced tempo sessions and intervals, are hard work and there's no escaping that fact, but it is not worth working yourself up about them. By all means listen to advice from other experienced trail runners, but do what you feel is right for you – both in terms of enjoyment and fitness. Try not to get overly caught up in interval versus fartlek training and instead focus on exploring the trails while working hard on them to improve your anaerobic fitness.

08
TRAIL FINDING: LOCATING AND STAYING ON THE TRAILS

By now you should be far more informed about what being a trail runner involves and how you can differentiate this running discipline from pounding the pavements as a road runner. Of the many differences, one aspect of trail running which can take a bit of getting used to is finding suitable trails that challenge you as a runner yet offer you the stunning scenery that is synonymous with trail running. Road runners have the advantage of simply putting on their kit and heading out of the front door – the biggest decision they have to make is whether to turn left or right.

Trail runners on the other hand often don't have this luxury. Unless you're lucky enough to live right next to a trail path or near a forest, it's likely you'll have to either run for a few miles before you find a trail or in some cases (particularly for city dwellers) drive to your nearest trail. As frustrating as this might be, once you have scoured your local area for a variety of routes, you'll be amazed at how many stunning trails are right on your doorstep – though finding them is the tricky part.

FINDING THE BEST TRAILS

In the early stages of your transition from the road to the trails, my advice would be to start out on trails that you know well and those you have experienced in the past. Whether you've been walking them with your dog, family or even experimented running on them in preparation for a road race, if you have intentions to progress your trail-running ambitions, stick with what you know for the first few weeks and get familiar with the terrain. As your fitness improves and your natural curiosity eventually gets the better of you, there are several ways to search for an appropriate trail route to suit your ability.

FORUMS AND SOCIAL MEDIA

Just a few simple Internet searches will lead you to a plethora of running and dedicated trail running websites, many with integrated forums and

platforms through which you can join the online community to exchange ideas, get tips and ask questions about trail routes in your region. If you live in the UK, for example, visit trailrunning.co.uk or goodrunguide.co.uk where you'll find forums to sign up to and ask fellow trail runners if anyone is familiar with your area and if they know of any scenic trail routes. The overwhelming majority of people who use these forums are incredibly helpful and if they can't help you directly, they'll often put you in touch with someone (or another website) who can. For US-based runners, friendly forums can be found at trailrunnernation.com and backcountryrunner.com.

As well as forums, social media sites such as Twitter and Facebook can also be very useful in engaging with people, magazines and companies all associated (and very much in love) with trail running. By liking a trail running Facebook page, such as facebook.com/TrailRunningMag for UK runners and facebook.com/trailrunnermag in the USA, it puts you in touch with a like-minded community. Simply by following the right people and organisations on Twitter can also open the door to a whole new world of people across the globe who can help you find a trail wherever you wish to run.

INTERACTIVE MAPPING WEBSITES

The evolution of GPS tracking devices has transformed the running world, with runners now being able to digitally log their training sessions and record a plethora of information such as average pace, heart rate, altitude and distance covered. Software companies have capitalised on the upsurge of interest and produced some fantastic user-friendly websites where you can not only upload and store all of your training data, but that data is then collated into a gargantuan database of

running routes (over 25 million) all over the world. By selecting a number of route criteria such as location, difficulty, surface, terrain, etc., the website searches its database and produces a selection of suitable routes.

Perhaps the most popular website of this type is mapmyrun.com, but there are many others available to runners. All the routes you find on this site have come directly from fellow trail runners, either via their GPS or by manual upload, so you can have confidence that these trails are bona fide and safe to negotiate. If you need further peace of mind, there are options on most websites to view the satellite images of the trail so you can see for yourself where it goes and what potential hazards you may have to look out for.

MAP READING

It might sound a little old-fashioned in light of modern technology and satellite imagery, but turning to a paper Ordnance Survey map and scouring it for suitable trail routes is another way to find a run near you. Of course, due to the wonders of the

FICKLE TRAILS

Even though a certain route is mapped and looks good to run on the satellite images, the fickle and changeable nature of trails throughout the seasons can make the going very different from one month to the next. Flood water, ice, snow or even dryness leading to scree (broken rock fragments at the bottom of a hill) can make running a trail a very different experience each time. My advice is to be aware of local weather conditions and on your first outing, always run a trail cautiously until you become more familiar with it.

>> *The red arrow points north*

Internet most paper maps are now also available as PDF downloads from mapping organisations such as Ordnance Survey (ordnancesurvey.co.uk) in the UK and USGS (US Geological Survey: usgs.gov) in the USA.

Regardless of how you access them, learning how to read maps is an incredibly useful skill to acquire if you're going to be spending time on remote trail routes. Proficiency in map reading is a skill learned over time, yet one that I strongly advise you to pursue if you have long-term trail-running goals.

LEARNING A NEW LANGUAGE

Learning to translate what the map is telling you is a little bit like learning a different language – some people get to grips with it faster than others. Once you have grasped the basic concepts, life on the long trail runs can get really interesting – and a heck of a lot more fun and adventurous.

Not only will being able to read the topography of any terrain increase your confidence on the trails, but it also gives you the peace of mind that you know exactly where you are at any given time. In addition, map-reading skills also provide you with a safety assurance that if you injure yourself and need to call for help, you can locate your position on the map and give the respective coordinates to people who will come to your aid (see also page 34).

On the basis that entire publications are dedicated to teaching you how to read maps, I won't go into detail here. There are some excellent map reading and navigational books available to purchase and I strongly suggest you look into purchasing one to help you make the most out of trail running in unfamiliar surroundings. Good books worth considering are *The Collins Ultimate Navigation Manual* by Lyle Brotherton (Collins) or *Navigation: Using Your Map and Compass* by Pete Hawkins (Cicerone Press).

COMPASS READING

As useful as map reading is, knowing how to identify, for example, certain landmarks and gradients on a map is only partially useful if you don't know which direction you are running in. This is where another reading skill can come in incredibly handy – using a compass.

Unless you were a member of the Boy Scouts or Girl Guides or had parents who were very much into walking in the wilderness when you were young, it's unlikely you'll have been taught how to use a compass for navigational purposes. Like map reading, learning to read a compass is an essential skill for any serious trail runner. In my opinion, whether you anticipate running in your local area or further afield, learning the basics of compass reading is a smart move, as it simply gives you another safety measure if/when you get into trouble.

THE BASICS

As patronisingly obvious as it might be, the picture opposite shows the four main points of a compass: north, south, east and west. In between each point is a further bearing, collectively known as intermediate directions; for example, between north and east is north-east and between south and west is south-west, and so on.

For 99 per cent of readers, this information is obvious and basic general knowledge. **However, this fact doesn't stop trail runners running in the wrong direction.** In fact, it happens far more often than you might think.

Learning to read a compass and run in a certain direction on a bearing can be tricky when you first start and mistakes are easily made. By practising your navigational skills on every training run, whether or not they are required, you'll get to grips with a compass and become familiar with some of the more common navigational mistakes.

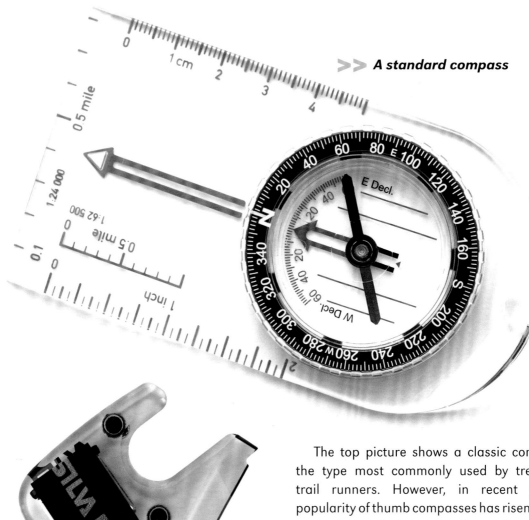

>> *A standard compass*

>> *A thumb compass*

The top picture shows a classic compass and the type most commonly used by trekkers and trail runners. However, in recent years the popularity of thumb compasses has risen with many runners negotiating unfamiliar trail routes. Their diminutive design and accuracy are just as reliable as conventional compasses, so there's no reason why your first/next compass can't fit nicely on your thumb.

Whichever model you choose, it counts for nothing unless you can use it, so here are your first steps towards learning how to run on a bearing.

LESSON 1: THE ARROW POINTS NORTH

I could almost leave lesson 1 at that. The needle always points north, no matter what direction you are running. The potential stumbling block is that compass arrows have two ends, so it's important to know that in the vast majority of cases it is the **RED** arrow that points north. It's not uncommon for some compasses to add an extra reminder of this fact by also placing a big '**N**' on the RED arrow as well, just to make sure you don't make the mistake of walking south (which can and does happen far more often than you'd think – so don't get complacent).

LESSON 2: RUNNING IN OTHER DIRECTIONS

If the only direction you want to run is north, stop at lesson 1! However, assuming you'd like to change direction/bearing fairly regularly, you'll need to learn how to use the compass to point you in the right direction. For the sake of argument, let's say you'd like to travel west.

See the 'housing' that covers the arrow? You'll notice you can turn it all the way round. Once you've rotated the housing you'll also notice that there are two bold parallel lines in the middle of the base (along with others on either side). This is the key; in order to run in the direction you wish to travel, in this case west, you need to rotate the housing so that the '**W**' (west) letter lines up with the '**direction of travel**' arrow, which is located on the main base of the compass. Once they are aligned, hold the compass flat with the direction of travel arrow pointing away from you and slowly rotate your body until the **RED** arrow sits neatly inside those two parallel lines inside the compass housing (*see* Figure 8.2).

>> *Maps don't run out of battery*

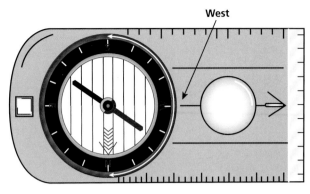

>> *Figure 8.1 Travelling west*

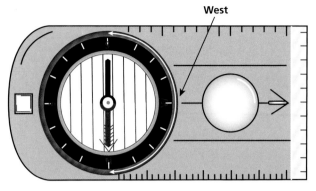

>> *Figure 8.2 Lining up your direction of travel*

I cannot stress the importance of checking and double-checking that the RED arrow is pointing north. If you find yourself in a hurry, it is easy to make the error of having the **BLACK** arrow pointing north, leaving you setting off in completely the wrong direction. Once you're sure everything is correct, set off running in a westerly direction with the peace of mind that you're heading the right way.

LESSON 3: INTEGRATING A MAP

Once you have confidently mastered the skill of running in all directions of the compass, the next step is to be able to read a map, see a landmark

SPANNER IN THE WORKS

Due to the sensitivity of the arrow to anything metallic, interference can be problematic and lead to inaccurate readings. If you think your arrow is behaving in a haphazard or erratic manner, make sure there is nothing metallic in the near vicinity, such as in your backpack or even your watch. Remove any suspect items, then retry to see if that makes a difference and provides you with a more accurate reading.

you wish to get to and run on the right bearing in order to get there safely. For whatever reason – be it adventure, making a short cut or the need to get help fast – you find yourself at point **A** on the map and needing to get to point **B**. Here's what you do:

- **Step 1:** Line up points **A** and **B** along the edge of the compass base. Make sure the 'direction of travel arrow' is pointing **FROM** point **A** (where you are standing) **TO** point **B** (where you wish to go).
- **Step 2:** Align the lines within the compass housing (*see* Figure 8.2) so they run parallel with the north running lines on the map by rotating the housing, so that the '**N**' mark on the housing is pointing to the top of the map.
- **Step 3:** Re-check the edge of the compass to make sure it is aligned with points A and B and again check that the orienteering lines within the compass housing run parallel with the north running lines on the map.
- **Step 4:** Take the compass off the map and, keeping it very still and flat with the direction of travel arrow pointing away from you (as recommended in lesson 2), slowly rotate your body and compass until the **RED** arrow is aligned nicely within the centre lines of the compass housing.

- **Step 5:** When you have everything aligned, it is important to ensure the compass housing does not move or you'll end up walking off course. If possible, when you have your bearing and you know the direction you should be travelling, look into the distance for a landmark of some description and run towards that. This way, even if the housing is accidentally moved, you know you're heading in the right direction.

>> *Getting from A to B using your smartphone*

VANISHING TRAILS

Although some people have absolutely no intention of incorporating these navigational techniques into their trail-running adventures, some will thrive on such challenges. Using compass and map reading techniques to run off your usual route can be fun, but be aware that what starts as a pleasant run on a familiar trail can end up more akin with a cross country or even fell run if the terrain is particularly tricky. To that end, unless you are very familiar with the area, leave heading out for a trail run and navigating off track to random points on a map until you are of a high level of fitness and have complete confidence in your navigational capabilities.

APPS
MAP APPS

If all this sounds either a little too complicated or simply old-fashioned, you always have the choice of embracing modern technology and letting your smartphone do the work for you. Although poor signal, battery life and a fatal intolerance to wet weather might well be sufficiently good reasons to reconsider relying totally on your iPhone or Android phone, there are a wide range of user-friendly apps available to buy which are there to make your life a little easier. While you must take into account the limitations of mapping apps, particularly when it comes to battery life, their functionality, accuracy and low cost make them viable options, or additions, to your map and compass.

With factors such as improved mobile reception and software development, many apps listed at the time of writing may well already be outdated, but

to help give you an idea of what they can offer you, here are two that are well worth considering.

VIEWRANGER
viewranger.com
Perhaps the best value and most functional app you can buy is Viewranger.

Viewranger essentially turns your smartphone into a GPS navigator and gives you a vast range of navigational functions that are ideally suited to trail runners. When used in conjunction with the website, you can find, plan, record and view a range of trails wherever you are in the world, and with the ability to download and store maps to your smartphone, you needn't worry if the mobile signal is weak or non-existent.

With the option to download highly detailed Ordnance Survey maps, Viewranger is one app you should seriously consider installing on to your smartphone – even if you have no intention of using its full range of functions. If you only have it on standby as a safety resource, the small amount of money you spend on this app will be worth its weight in gold should you find yourself in trouble out on the trails.

TWONAV

compegps.com

Presented in a slightly different way than Viewranger but certainly not lacking in function, TwoNav provides trail runners with a wide range of maps to view and track as well as a helpful compass embedded in the interface. Like most other top-end GPS apps, you have the ability to track your routes and upload them to other websites for either your own training records – or for bragging purposes.

If you like detail and feedback while out training, TwoNav offers you a very impressive number of stats on your run including your altitude, coordinates, sunset/sunrise time, heart rate (with compatible strap) and speed. A total of 70 details about your run are available to view, making this app heaven for the feedback hungry among you.

WORD OF WARNING

As fun and as useful as these features are, remember that as a general rule, the more features an app has the more battery hungry it will be. Although this won't generally be an issue for trail runs lasting a couple of hours, if you plan to be out all afternoon, bear in mind that towards the end of the day the battery on your smartphone will start to run low.

As a safeguard, if you find your battery is getting low and you're still a fair way from home, turn your phone off when your battery reaches 10 per cent power and use an alternative form of navigation. You should always ensure that you have enough power to use your phone should you need to make an emergency call or, at the very least, send a text.

By all means make the most of the advances in modern technology, but it's best not to become over-reliant on them. By learning the traditional skills of map and compass reading in this chapter, you have the best of both worlds on hand. You never know when they might come in handy.

09

THE ELEMENTS: EXTREME TRAIL-RUNNING CONDITIONS

Whatever terrain or running discipline you choose, whether it is road running, fell running, cross country or indeed trail training, racing in extreme weather conditions is all part of the allure and the challenge of the sport.

From the freezing cold to the sizzling heat, weather extremes are incredibly exhilarating conditions to run in, and when you factor in miles of unpredictable trail paths, the subsequent adrenaline coursing through your veins only reinforces your justification for swapping the road for the trails. While being in Mother Nature's playground when she's in a bad mood can hook you into trail running for years to come, it is important to be aware of the effect that certain running conditions can have on your body.

In the early days of your trail running adventures when your trail runs are often short and close to home, it's unlikely you'll be out on the trails long enough to worry too much if you're caught out by changeable or extreme conditions. However, as time goes on and you venture further afield, you'll need to be far more vigilant.

Making seasonal preparations naturally depends on where it is you'll be trail running. Winter trail running in the UK, where you can expect snow, ice and high winds, is a very different experience compared to, say, Southern California or Sydney, where winter conditions are usually far more temperate in comparison.

If you live in the UK and/or plan to run the plethora of trails in England, Ireland, Scotland, Wales or indeed anywhere in northern Europe, ensuring you have the right kit in your wardrobe for every season and weather condition makes training safer and therefore more enjoyable. Therefore, take the financial hit early on and never head out on the trails wearing inappropriate kit.

TRAILING IN THE HEAT

Running in the heat places obvious demands on the body. Increased levels of perspiration, elevated heart rate and premature fatigue are all common symptoms of running in warm conditions, but how

much do these symptoms affect performance? What measures can you take to help cool yourself down? When should we be concerned that the heat is getting the better of us?

- **Fact 1:** Running in extreme heat is oppressive and it can take some getting used to.
- **Fact 2:** The human body is an ingenious machine and is capable of adapting to whatever conditions you make it run in – even if the temperature soars.

AVOID THE 'IT'LL DO' APPROACH

We've all done it and we have all regretted it at one time or another, yet some of us never learn. You're all ready for a run and itching to head out the door when you suddenly realise your vest, base layer, long-sleeve top or gloves are in the wash. It is easier to get away with the 'Oh, it'll do' approach on shorter runs, but you will often regret your choice in extreme conditions.

A classic clothing 'It'll do' scenario is throwing on a long-sleeve top instead of a vest. It may not seem like the greatest sin at the time, but when you're out running for a few hours in high temperatures and fully kitted up, the extra heat you retain will slowly hinder your performance and likely increase your rate of sweating and fluid loss. 'It'll do' is a small phrase with potentially big consequences for trail runners, so think twice before being flippant about your choice of training kit.

This is far from an invite for you to head out for a long trail run in the heat, banking on the fact that every system in your ingenious body will kick in and see you through a scorching training session in one piece – but your body is made to handle the heat.

Despite this natural physiological capacity, before you can cover miles and miles without feeling serious side effects, you've first of all got to encourage your body to adapt. This adaptation occurs far quicker for some runners than others, but regardless of individual variances, with the right amount of preparation and correct exposure to heat training everyone can encourage the body to tolerate running in hot conditions – you've just got to learn how.

COOLING DOWN

Offering a full and in-depth explanation of how the body regulates its core temperature during exercise is far more complex than many people realise. The body has an optimal functional temperature of between 36.1 and 37.8°C (97 and 100°F) and it does everything it can to keep you within this temperature range. The most common situations that can lead to a rise in core temperature include:

- Prolonged and intense periods of exercise
- Illness or fever
- Exposure to extreme heat (or cold)

At some stage you'll find yourself running in hot conditions, so you can bet your bottom dollar you'll tick two of the above (here's a clue – you should never exercise with a fever). Therefore, controlling your core body temperature and keeping it within the normal temperature range in warm conditions is key to your trail running success and preventing **hyperthermia**.

Contrary to popular belief, however, the process of sweating in itself is not the most effective way to

> **HYPERTHERMIA**
> This is the condition in which your core body temperature rises above normal levels, i.e. greater than 37.8°C (100°F).

keep the body's core temperature within safe limits – a fact that is well worth bearing in mind if you think the more you sweat, the better you're handling the conditions. Other heat loss mechanisms such as radiation, convection and conduction also have big roles to play, but for the purposes of this book we'll focus on the most important and easily controlled heat loss method: evaporation.

EVAPORATE TO TOLERATE

You don't have to be a runner to know that the process of sweating plays a key (though not definitive) role in assisting the body to cool down our internal core temperature when it starts rising. Sweating during training is a normal and (for runners) welcome bodily function. Although it is commonly used for many runners as a way to guage how hard they are working, sweating is only part one of the heat loss process and contributes very little to actually cooling us down. We can sweat as much as we like but our core body temperature continues to rise unless our sweat is turned into vapour, resulting in the much-needed loss of heat from our body via our skin. Armed with this basic physiological knowledge, as runners facing miles of hot trails in the middle of the day we must do everything we can to maximise the process of evaporation to keep us cool and ultimately keep us running.

There are a number of measures we can take to maximise sweat evaporation, which might not sound revolutionary, but attention to even the smallest details can make a big difference on long, hot training runs.

CLOTHING

Perhaps the most obvious step you can take is to ensure you wear as little as possible. By keeping the skin exposed to the air, any breeze that hits your skin will help to evaporate the sweat and keep your core temperature within normal limits. A (preferably white) hat is also vital to shield yourself from the sun.

However, there's a spanner in the works for trail runners: when wearing minimal clothing and a poor quality or inappropriate backpack, there is potential for a compromise in comfort from chafing, so always make sure you run a short distance with your backpack in hot weather clothing first before tackling a challenging two-hour run.

There are a range of highly breathable shorts and vests on the market. These include a mesh

fabric to help wick sweat away from the body and circulate air to encourage the evaporation process.

However, it is not just the fabric and the meshing which will help to keep you cool – but also the colour of your clothes. Remember: dark colours absorb heat from the sun, which only contributes to your heat stress. Always wear light colours such as white or light yellow as they help to reflect heat away from the body and keep you cool.

In recent years, there has been some discussion of the benefits of compression tops under loose fitting ones to help with heat regulation. The theory is that although compression vests hug the skin and don't allow air to circulate, they wick sweat away from the body to be evaporated, thus actually helping to keep you cool. The jury is still out on this one, so by all means trial both loose fitting and compression tops, but ultimately you've got to wear what you feel comfortable wearing.

CHOOSE YOUR ROUTE WISELY

If you have no option but to take to the trails for a training run in the middle of a hot day, then choosing the most appropriate route for the conditions can make a big difference to both your performance and safety.

As you become more familiar with the trails in your area, you'll often find there are a few that are either much more sheltered or a little more exposed to the open landscape. A sheltered route, such as

>> Run on shady routes if possible.

HUMIDITY

Taking sensible clothing and route precautions when you are trail running in dry heat is one thing, but when the atmosphere is humid and already saturated with upwards of 90 per cent water vapour, keeping cool is a far more challenging prospect. In high humidity, the air is already incredibly wet, which has a direct effect on the amount of sweat evaporating from the skin. The more humid the air, the less capacity it has to accept more water vapour, thereby significantly reducing the rate of sweat evaporation.

Therefore, running in hot and humid conditions is arguably the most challenging environment for a runner, as the body struggles to evaporate the huge quantities of sweat it secretes in a desperate attempt to cool the body down. Add to this the lack of a breeze and the risk of dehydration and overheating becomes a real factor.

If you have no option but to run in humid conditions, try to limit your sessions to one hour or less and carry at least 2–3l of electrolyte fluid with you (*see* Chapter 10).

a forest trail, will help to keep you out of direct sunlight and prevent the heat from becoming too oppressive. A route which is a little more exposed increases the chances of there being a breeze to help encourage your sweat to evaporate and keep you cool.

As minor as these precautions might seem, they actually go a long way towards ensuring your summer training sessions are much more bearable and, more importantly, safer.

HOW THE BODY ADAPTS TO HEAT

If you live in a hot country or, more importantly, if the conditions of your scheduled trail race are likely to be on the warm side, ensuring your body is conditioned for running in the heat is going to be far more effective for performance than putting on a white vest and hoping there will be some shade or a breeze.

Remember, the human body is incredibly good at adapting to whatever stresses you place it under. Asking it to tolerate running for miles and miles on a hot trail is no different. Although certain individuals will adapt better and faster than others, everyone is capable of encouraging the body to become more efficient when running in the heat, so as hard as hot weather training might be, try and stick with it.

Over the years, top athletes have tried a range of things to help encourage their body to tolerate heat when running, but whether you try wearing several layers to really crank up the heat stress on the body (not recommended) or just run regular bouts in the hottest part of the day, the best way to encourage the body to tolerate the heat is to run in the heat. Obvious, maybe, but before you head out of the door when the mercury hits 30°C (86°F), it's worth knowing exactly how your body will adapt to your warm weather training.

By exposing your body to the heat during a run, a series of systems and mediums are encouraged to help cool the body down for subsequent training runs. These include:

- The cardiovascular system
- The blood
- Sweat efficiency

THE CARDIOVASCULAR SYSTEM

By exposing the body to hot weather training over the course of several weeks, the cardiovascular system responds by reducing the working heart rate. The more training runs you perform, the more the body is able to tolerate the conditions and the less hard the heart needs to work. This reduction in heart rate helps to preserve energy, meaning that you'll be able to stay on the trails for longer without fatiguing prematurely.

The more efficient your heart rate, the more blood can be spared instead to go to the skin surface to help emit heat – this helps prevent your body temperature getting too high.

THE BLOOD

Heat acclimatisation has a massive influence on the blood. Leading physiologists Wilmore and Costill (*Physiology of Sport and Exercise,* 5th ed, Human Kinetics) found that after the first few days of heat training the volume of plasma in the blood expands.

This expansion assists the cardiovascular system in maintaining good cardiac output (the amount of blood pumped around the body every minute), in turn maintaining a good blood supply to the skin, which not only keeps your muscles moving but also radiates heat.

SWEAT EFFICIENCY

"Sweating removes between 1092 and 2520kj of heat per litre of sweat evaporated."
Tim Noakes, *Lore of Running,*
(Human Kinetics, 2003)

>> *Run in the heat regularly to build tolerance.*

The longer you spend acclimatising to the heat, the more your body will adapt to the conditions by increasing the amount you sweat. If you are training in high humidity where the evaporation of sweat is decreased, then increased sweating becomes even more important. Remember: although sweating itself can assist in cooling you down, it is the evaporation of that sweat which is far more important. Therefore, by increasing the amount you sweat you increase your body's ability to cool itself down.

Electrolytes are lost through sweating and passing urine. Although higher levels of electrolytes are lost through sweat in hot conditions, they can also be lost during cooler runs too. This reduces the risk of impeding muscle contractions (causing cramp) or serious conditions such as **hypernatremia** (*see* page 185).

HYDRATION: FIGHTING THE HEAT

In hot weather you could lose over 2l fluid for every hour you are running – so staying hydrated is crucial. Although experts in recent years have indicated there is often an over emphasis on the importance of taking on fluids when running, when it comes to training in the high temperatures, every effort and precaution must be taken to ensure your fluid levels are replaced.

There are lots of reasons for this (see Chapter 11) but for me the most important is because of the positive effect it has on blood plasma.

Blood plasma makes up around half the total volume of the blood and when you consider that plasma is made up of 92 per cent water, you don't need to be a scientist to understand just how important water is to the blood. The increased amount of sweat you produce when running in hot conditions slowly decreases the plasma's water percentage, gradually causing your blood to become thick and more viscous. Your blood is still able to carry out its roles of supplying essential nutrients and oxygen to the working muscles, but as dehydration sets in and your blood becomes thicker, your heart is made to work harder to push that more viscous substance around the body. This causes an increased heart rate and the potential for premature fatigue.

If you're planning to be out on the trails for several hours then dehydration and its effect on your performance and health can be a serious problem, so always ensure your hydration pack is full whenever you run in the heat.

HEAT ILLNESS: THE WARNING SIGNS

When running long distances in high temperatures, unless you are showing signs of hyperthermia (*see* page 139), you are always going to feel warm and at times uncomfortable, as your body works overtime to keep you cool and functioning at a high running intensity.

For the vast majority of time spent running in heat, your symptoms may include feeling warm, your breathing will be laboured with an elevated heart rate and increased amount of perspiration. Although you'll finish the trail exhausted, a good rest and adequate hydration should make you feel better in no time. However, it is important to learn to recognise when the body is struggling to cope with the heat and exercise demands.

The following diagram lists the common symptoms often associated with heat stress. These conditions are listed in order of severity, with the first of the symptoms indicating early signs of heat stress, progressing to the more severe signs of heat stroke.

TREATING HEAT-RELATED ILLNESS

Ultimately, preventing any form of heat illness is your first priority. Taking all necessary measures to keep your body as cool as possible should always be at the forefront of your mind, but if you or a running partner experience any of the symptoms in figure 9.1, it is essential you take immediate action to cool yourself or your buddy down.

In an ideal world, if your body begins to experience the common signs of heat exhaustion – such as nausea, goose bumps and headaches – the first measure you'd take is to stop running immediately, go into a cool environment and encourage the blood to return to the heart by lying on your back with your legs raised. Needless to say, finding yourself an hour's run from civilisation with symptoms of heat exhaustion is not an ideal world situation, so what should you do if you're in this predicament?

1. Stop immediately

First and foremost, stop. For the competitive among you, this might be difficult, but in the interests of your health (and possibly life) you must stop running immediately.

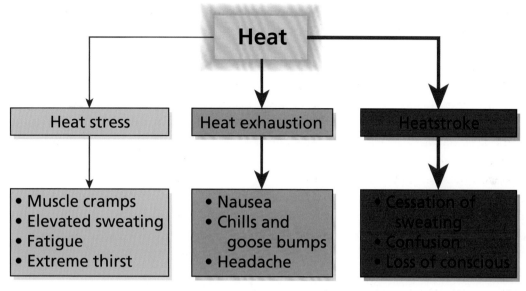

>> *Figure 9.1 The signs of heat illness*

2. Increase air circulation

Next, remove your backpack and/or top to help circulate air around your body to aid sweat evaporation. Find some shade if you can and breathe steadily. Calm your whole body down and try to relax.

3. Rehydrate

Take on fluids from your bottles and/or backpack bladder. Rehydrating is essential to reduce your core body temperature, so take small and regular sips.

Provided you have caught the signs of heat illness in the early stages and you are able to find shade (and hopefully a breeze) to help cool you down and of course replace lost fluids, there is no reason why you shouldn't be able to carry on running gently after 10–15 minutes or so. Although the most preferable solution would be to hail a cab and get back home to recuperate, on the basis that there aren't many cabs on remote trail paths, you'll have little option but to carry on – or, indeed, turn back if it's closer.

HEATSTROKE

Occurs when your core temperature exceeds 40.6°C due to heat exposure. It is a far more serious condition than heat exhaustion and urgent medical attention is required to help replace fluids and cool the body down. It is advised that anyone suffering from symptoms of heatstroke should be moved into a cool area and if possible immersed in cool water.

If in the rare situation you find yourself with the more severe symptoms of heat stroke, such as being in a state of confusion, disorientation and/or sleepy, it is essential you call someone immediately and tell them your location as best you can. Find shade and follow all the steps above to get your body temperature down.

RESPECT THE HEAT

For all the clothing and training precautions you can take to build up a tolerance to hot weather running, ultimately you have to learn to respect the conditions. As trail runners running on remote paths, we are that much more vulnerable to weather conditions and it is easy to let them get the better of you. Although hyperthermia and the symptoms associated with it may not necessarily stop you in your tracks, the more serious condition of heat stroke certainly will, so always listen to your body and take every precaution you can. Always take plenty of fluids with you on the trail and tell someone where you are going and how long you plan to be. The challenge of running in the heat can be exhilarating; just don't let exhilaration turn into desperation.

TRAILING IN THE COLD

At the other extreme, running in the cold presents a new set of challenges to trail runners. In the majority of cases, the risks of running in the heat are far greater than running in the cold, but the dangers of **hypothermia** are real for anyone planning to run long distance in the winter, so never underestimate the importance of taking the right precautions.

HYPOTHERMIA

This is the condition in which your core body temperature drops below functioning levels, i.e. less than 35°C (95°F).

>> *Trail running in the snow can be magical.*

STAYING WARM

When you're running in cold weather, provided you're appropriately dressed, then the body's natural production of heat can be to your benefit. Heat produced by our working muscles helps to counteract the cold atmospheric conditions we'll experience on a long sub-zero trail run, preventing a drop in body temperature. However, this is not the full story and it is essential to understand how the body adapts and responds to cold weather before embarking on a long training run on an icy trail path.

Like the heat, cold conditions vary greatly depending on a number of factors. One cold day is not necessarily the same as another, even though the mercury gives you the same reading. This variability in conditions can influence our ability to stay warm so never assume one cold run will be the same as another. Wind chill, cloud cover and sunshine have a significant influence on how the body responds to the conditions, so irrespective of what the thermometer says, a 10-mile trail run in -5°C (23°F) in the sunshine is a very different proposition to one on a hill trail in exposed and windy conditions. Take note of the details of the weather conditions.

COLD SWEATS

Choosing what to wear for a cold weather run is crucial in keeping your core body temperature within its normal limits, but it's harder than it would first seem. The conditions might initially feel worthy of several layers as you head out in the cold and wind, but as you progress through the run and your body slowly warms up, you'll need to peel off the layers to cool down.

Think about the following scenario: it's a cold morning and you've got a 15-mile trail run to do in cold and windy conditions. Your immediate instinct, quite understandably, is to wrap up in several layers to ensure you'll stay warm for the entirety

THE INTENSITY FACTOR

The intensity of your planned trail run in the cold should play a key role in both your choice of clothing and the potential risks of contracting hypothermia.

The more intense your planned run (be it speed or steep inclines) the more your body heats up and, therefore, the more sweat you will produce.

Ultimately you have to remember that we are all different and sweat at different rates. Although larger runners will generally produce more sweat than smaller framed runners, it's a dangerous game to play if you simply follow rules of thumb. Experiment with different types and quantities of clothes on short runs first and find that balance between feeling too hot and too cold.

of the run. Perversely, it is those extra layers which could actually contribute to a significant drop in core body temperature. As your muscle contraction increases, so too does your core temperature, leading to heavy sweat. The layers further capture the sweat and this extra moisture causes you to lose heat at a fast rate. This might be ideal in hot conditions, but is not so great when the wind is blowing Arctic air at you. So, although I'm far from suggesting you head out into the cold with nothing but a vest and shorts, you should be aware of the dangers of wearing too many clothes. You'll have to accept you'll be on the chilly side for the first 10 minutes or so, but you'll soon warm up and enjoy the rest of your run at the perfect temperature (see Chapter 2 for more on investing in good quality cold weather running kit).

EXTREMITIES

Working out the correct number of layers to wear in cold conditions can often take a few attempts, especially if you are new to running in the cold, but fortunately looking after your extremities is far easier.

>> *Waterproof shoes are ideal for snowy trails.*

During exercise, your working muscles demand high quantities of blood to provide them with all the oxygen and nutrients they need to meet the demands of the run. In cold weather, the blood flow to your extremities, including your fingers, toes, ears and nose, is reduced, diverted instead to the major muscles. The result of this reduced blood flow is cold extremities, which over the course of a long run can be very uncomfortable, particularly for the fingers. In temperate conditions, you don't tend to be aware of the reduced blood flow to your extremities as the ambient temperature is warm enough to keep them happy, but turn the temperature down and that lack of blood becomes an uncomfortable issue. You'll be thankful you added a pair of gloves and a hat to your winter weather trail running kit.

THE PHYSIOLOGICAL EFFECTS OF THE COLD

Provided you have got your clothing right and your extremities are protected from the biting cold, trail running in the winter can be an invigorating experience. The scenery and tranquillity of running on trails covered with virgin snow combine to give

GETTING COLD FEET?

You could argue that of all the extremities, the feet get the best deal. Protected from the cold by a pair of socks and a pair of shoes, they are snuggled up in two layers and can enjoy a long trail run without feeling the effects of the cold, despite suffering from a slightly reduced blood flow.

While this may be true in some circumstances, throw in a trail run on a path ankle-deep in snow and all that goes out of the window. The accumulation of melted snow will eventually saturate your shoes, socks and ultimately your toes, which could lead to a very uncomfortable run and even the possibility of frostbite.

In these conditions, you have a few of options. First, you can either invest in a pair of waterproof trail shoes, which should prevent moisture from entering the shoe. Second, some runners wrap duct tape around the meshing at the front of their shoe to prevent moisture seeping in. Finally, carry several pairs of extra socks with you and stop to change them every now and again – it's not an ideal situation, but it is far more preferable to putting up with cold and wet feet on a long run.

you an uplifting, even spiritual experience, but if you intend to spend any length of time out in those conditions, there are one or two things you should be aware of. The physiological effects of cold weather trail running may not necessarily affect you in the early stages of training, but as the miles creep up the following facts are certainly worth knowing.

- Extreme shivering can produce heat at a rate five times greater than your base metabolic rate. It is possible to stop yourself shivering... for a bit. Eventually, your body over-rules you and you will have no control over your rate of shivering.
- During prolonged exercise in cold conditions, the body may actually lose heat faster than in more temperate conditions. As the muscles demand more blood to keep working, it is diverted away from the core, thereby accelerating heat loss.
- Your hypothalamus regulates your body temperature, but if it drops below 34.5°C (94.1°F), it struggles to keep control. When core body temperature drops below 30°C (85°F), control is lost completely and external factors must help heat you up.
- Incidences of exercise-induced asthma are higher in runners who train at a high intensity in cold conditions.

While in practical terms you have little or no control over most of these physiological functions, it is worth looking at some of the functions mentioned above in more detail.

MUSCLE FUNCTION

Your key aim in any run, whether in the heat or cold, is to keep your muscles functioning at the required intensity for the run's duration, especially if you are training your body to adapt to longer and harder trail runs. Provided the muscles are firing well and feeling fresh, they are able to keep the metabolism ticking over and therefore maintain a good production of heat. However, if the muscles start to fatigue they contract less and you start to slow down, meaning your core temperature drops. This is especially dangerous on a cold run when you are at the limits of your endurance capability. As your core temperature continues to drop, your fatigue levels increase as the body is simply unable to produce the heat necessary to keep the body warm. By using your common sense and wearing the right kit for the conditions, you can help to prevent this type of of drop in body temperature.

EXERCISE-INDUCED ASTHMA

Even runners who have had no previous experience of asthma may find that running in cold conditions can trigger an episode of exercise-induced asthma, as the lining of the respiratory airways can go into spasm. Although not usually serious, it can be a nasty shock when these spasms occur, so understanding the symptoms and treatment for such attacks is essential if you plan running in very cold weather.

As you inhale cold and dry air it can constrict sensitive bronchial airways and close up the air passages, resulting in symptoms of asthma. The first attack can often come as a complete surprise to people who have never suffered from asthma before but there are several steps you can take to reduce your chances of an attack.

When you consider that it is the dryness and the coldness of the air which contributes to narrowing your airways, inhaling large volumes of air very quickly will increase the risk of an attack. As a runner, the demands of trail running naturally increases your rate of respiration and therefore the amount of air you inhale every minute. Although your body and airways will be able to tolerate a degree of constriction from the cold and dry air, for those who are predisposed to exercise-induced asthma, it's a wise move to avoid high-intensity training sessions in the cold to limit the narrowing of the air passages. To reduce your chances of an attack keep the intensity of running low and increase the pace of your run very gradually.

Remember: your body is smart and it counters the inhaled cold air by warming it up as soon as it enters the airway. In moderately cold weather, the body is able to warm up the inhaled air by at least 10–15°C (50–59°F) by the time it has reached your respiratory tract, thereby reducing airway constriction. However, in very cold conditions (-5°C/23°F and colder) you must be cautious. Stick with steady and moderately paced training sessions on very cold days and if you find that you are experiencing asthmatic symptoms, it might be a good idea to visit your GP who may consider prescribing you some broncho-dilating medication to help those wind pipes open up and prevent asthma attacks.

TRACTION CONTROL

Although it's a little patronising to tell you to be careful when running on cold and icy trail paths, it is still very easy to get complacent. Unlike footpaths and roads, which are often well gritted in snowy and icy conditions giving you plenty of traction underfoot, trail paths are untreated and are a haven for hidden ice patches. Frozen exposed tree roots, iced-over puddles and treacherously slippery rocks are waiting for you round every corner, so never be tempted to think that just because the first few miles of a trail are safe, the entire path will be free from hazards.

It's inevitable that at some stage you'll be caught unawares. Follow these simple steps to see you through your run in once piece:

- **Shorten your stride:** The shorter the stride, the more control you will have of your legs if/when you slide and the greater chance you have of preventing muscular or ligament injuries.
- **Lean forwards:** If you run with a very upright posture, try leaning forwards from the waist ever so slightly. Like shortening your stride, this will help to give you a little more control should you find yourself slipping and sliding.
- **Don't risk it:** In the ice and snow where certain hazards may not be immediately visible, don't take the risk of lunging or jumping on to objects which may very well be covered in hidden ice.

TRAILING AT ALTITUDE

If you really get the trail running bug there's a chance you'll find yourself taking a brutal trail run halfway up a mountain. As much as I encourage you to strive for these challenges and experience these incredible landscapes, it's worth getting to grips with the safeguards you must take before you run at altitude. Along with familiarising yourself with these precautions, it will also help to understand a few basic physiological principles of running at altitude.

REACHING NEW HEIGHTS

The one question I'm asked most frequently by many runners, both road and trail, is at what height above sea level does altitude become a factor in running performance – how high does the hill/mountain have to be before I can expect my body

>> *Running in the clouds creates its own risks.*

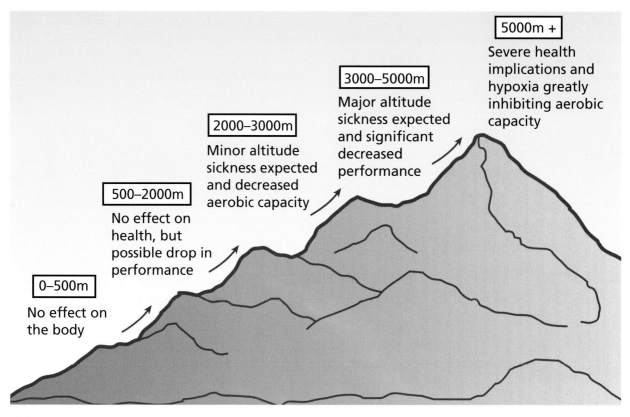

5000m +
Severe health implications and hypoxia greatly inhibiting aerobic capacity

3000–5000m
Major altitude sickness expected and significant decreased performance

2000–3000m
Minor altitude sickness expected and decreased aerobic capacity

500–2000m
No effect on health, but possible drop in performance

0–500m
No effect on the body

>> *Figure 9.2 The effects of altitude on running performance*

to start objecting about the lack of oxygen, resulting fatigue, headaches, nausea and general loss of sense of humour? *See* Figure 9.2 for the answer.

PHYSIOLOGICAL EFFECT OF RUNNING AT ALTITUDE

As a trail runner you're unlikely to venture above 2000m on a regular basis, but it's worth knowing what effects the lower altitudes can have on your body, how to prepare for it and how to spot the signs of altitude related ill health.

THE BIG OXYGEN MYTH

It is widely believed by many that the higher we go, the less oxygen is available in the air to breathe. Why else would those mountaineers climbing Everest need to wear oxygen masks? In actual fact, this is a myth and no matter where you are, from a Californian beach to the top of Mount Everest, the air always contains 20.93 per cent of oxygen. Breathing becomes more laboured because the higher we climb, the lower the air pressure.

This drop in air pressure (approximately 250mmHG at the summit of Everest and 760mmHG at sea level) significantly affects the transfer of oxygen to the lungs, and, therefore, its subsequent journey into the bloodstream and into the muscles. In short, the higher you go, the harder time the body has transporting and utilising oxygen. As a result, the muscles do not get the oxygen they need to continue functioning properly and fatigue can quickly set in. For the majority of trail runners, the effect of this change in air pressure won't be so dramatic that you notice the difference immediately, but over the course of a long-distance run you will certainly feel the effects.

So what should you expect when you train or race at altitude? Even at heights above 500m (1500ft) your heart, lungs and legs can expect a harder time than at sea level, so make sure you are fully aware of what to expect and adjust your expectations accordingly.

Altitude and performance

As seen in Figure 9.2, you should not experience any detrimental effects on your performance or functional heart rate at any given intensity on trail runs below 500m (about 1500ft). The air pressure at this relatively low altitude is sufficient to ensure your lungs can take in and use the oxygen in the air to keep you running at the intensity you like. Go significantly above 500m, however, and there is a chance you could start to notice subtle changes in the way you perform and how your body responds to a gradual reduction in atmospheric pressure. When you reach heights of 1500m and above, this is where you will certainly begin to notice a detrimental effect on your running performance and may experience the following physical and physiological changes:

- **Increased respiration:** Due to the lungs having to work harder to draw in the oxygen required to maintain running performance, you'll increase your breathing rate.
- **Increased heart rate:** As the body struggles to deliver sufficient oxygen to the muscles, the heart rate increases in an attempt to meet the oxygen demands.
- **Increased use of carbohydrate:** To meet the higher demands, the body needs easily available energy to fuel performance, so the body uses more carbohydrates.

- **Dehydration:** At altitudes above 1500–2000m, our bodies have a tendency to lose fluid more easily, especially during exercise. Therefore runners must be particularly vigilant about their fluid consumption and aim to drink upwards of 3–5l a day.

ADAPTING TO ALTITUDE

Over the years, a lot has been written in the press about the positive fitness benefits that can be achieved through training at altitude. This, in part, is due to the increased production of EPO, triggered by the low pressure of oxygen in the atmosphere, which increases the amount of red blood cells to help provide the working muscles with more oxygen. This benefit, however, is made more complicated by the fact that runners are unable to run at the same intensities as at sea level, thereby the effects even out.

For those trail runners unlikely to spend long periods of time at altitude, you are highly unlikely to improve your performance and fitness as a result of training at heights above 2000m. In fact, the time you spend running at these heights will almost certainly have a detrimental effect on your running fitness and ability, as explained above.

If you are planning on venturing up a mountain for a trail run, beware of the effect the altitude and reduced air pressure will have on your performance and make provisions to try to tolerate this impact. As long as you are aware that your heart rate will be higher, your breathing more laboured, you'll need more fluids and carbohydrate-rich snacks, you'll be well prepared to handle the effects of altitude.

10

TRAIL-RUNNING NUTRITION

You can train as hard as you like and strive to be the best runner you can be, but without eating right you'll fail to provide your body with adequate or sufficient nutrients to compliment training rigours. As obvious as this might sound, there is no one size fits all eating plan to suit every trail runner, and you won't get what you need if you simply copy a friend's eating plan or follow one you pulled out of a magazine. Moreover, there is a constant and ever-changing debate in the sports nutrition world as to what constitutes a performance-enhancing diet.

PERSONALISING YOUR NUTRITION

Nutritional rules are always in flux, let's look at current thinking and some fairly new theories too.

CARBOHYDRATES – TRAIL FUEL

Most runners reading this book will base their running diet on carbohydrates and will be successful in that approach – most nutritionists believe it should serve as your predominant source of energy on the trails.

When you exercise, the body accesses carbohydrate stored in your liver and muscles to help provide fuel for the legs and energy to see you safely through intense exercise periods. Your body is unable to break down alternative forms of energy (such as protein and fat)

fast enough to be successfully used as a fuel source, ultimately causing you to slow down, lack energy and generally feel fatigued. Therefore, as a trail runner, it is not only the consumption of carbohydrate which you should be vigilant about before, during and after a run, but the quantity of carbohydrate you consume is equally as important. It's all very well knowing that you need to put unleaded petrol in your car – but what use is it if you don't fill up the tank with enough fuel to get you from A to B? Good sources of carbohydrate can be found in table 10.3 on p.165.

TOO MUCH VERSUS TOO LITTLE

Once again, individuality is key when trying to figure out how much carbohydrate you need to fuel your

>> *Carbohydrate – trail fuel*

trail-running adventures. Although the formulae for calculating your carbohydrate needs are generally very accurate and suitable for most people, do not be lead into the false belief that they are written in stone and cannot be amended. There's every chance that you may need more or less carbohydrate than these formulae suggest, so feel free to amend these calculations to suit your individual needs. There are two tell-tale signs that suggest you might need to adjust your carbohydrate intake depending on whether you have too few or too many carbohydrates:

1. TOO LITTLE?

The most obvious sign you're not getting enough carbohydrate is if at the end of a long run you feel lacklustre, low in energy and like you're wearing lead shoes. Although a carbohydrate-rich drink or gel might give you a boost for a while, if you start to feel laboured in your running it could be a sign that you're not taking on sufficient amounts of carbohydrate before and after a training run. If you suspect this is the case, increase your intake and see how you get on. Some people burn carbohydrate at a faster rate than others (this author in particular), so don't be afraid to challenge the levels suggested over the page.

2. TOO MUCH?

The most obvious sign of excessive carbohydrate consumption for anyone, let alone trail runners, is weight gain. If you are taking on more energy than you are expending both from normal everyday physiological functions and training, the body will simply store that energy as fat. If you notice your weight is increasing despite an increase in training, consider revising your carbohydrate consumption and see if it helps to redress the energy balance.

Weight gain (or lack of weight loss) are of course not the only symptoms of eating excessive amounts of carbohydrate and/or the wrong type

of carbohydrate; the body's insulin response to carbohydrates is a complex subject and can result in weight gain or difficulties in losing weight, so by all means seek further information. However, one point that is certainly worth making is that running regularly can significantly help regulate the secretion of insulin and therefore blood sugar, so if you do overdo the carbs once in a while, it's a good job you're clocking up these miles to keep everything nice and balanced.

THE CARBOHYDRATE FORMULAE

Over the years, experts have tried to come up with the perfect formula to help runners work out what their daily consumption of carbohydrate should be, but theories and suggested levels tend to differ from one expert to the next. This is hardly surprising. Once again, it really depends on each individual so use the formulae as a guide only to judge how many carbohydrates you need.

To complicate things further, there are different formulae depending on what stage of training you are at: post-training, mid-training and pre-training. Exercise, particularly long duration and/or high-intensity exercise, initiates a complex series of hormonal reactions within the body. These hormonal secretions stimulate the muscles and liver to increase its ability to both use carbohydrate (during training) and then absorb it to maximise the replenishment of carbohydrate (post exercise) during your recovery. The trick is to ensure you give the body the correct quantities of carbohydrate at the right time so that come your next training run, your glycogen stores are topped up and ready to provide you with the energy necessary to tackle the long trail run ahead of you.

So, with that mind, use the following formulae to give you an idea of how much carbohydrate you should be looking to consume at any given stage of your training.

CARBOHYDRATES POST-TRAINING

Arguably the most important time to replenish carbohydrate stocks is after a training run. In the first few hours post run, your body secretes a hormone called **glycogenase**, which helps to maximise the body's ability to absorb and store away any carbohydrate-rich foods you consume. This ensures that your liver and muscles are well replenished, ready for your next training session.

According to leading sports dieticians Deakin and Burke, (*Clinical Sports Nutrition*, 2nd ed, McGraw-Hill), ideally you should be looking to use the following formula to work out how much carbohydrate you should be eating post run:

- **Immediately after exercise:** 1–1.5g of carbohydrate per kg of bodyweight. For example, if you weigh 70kg, you should aim to consume 70–105g of carbohydrate (this is the equivalent to one bagel or 2–3 large bananas).
- **In 24 hours after exercise:** 7–10g of carbohydrate per kg of bodyweight. For example, if you weigh 70kg, you should aim to consume 490–700g of carbohydrate. To give you a rough idea, if your chosen carbohydrate source is rice or pasta, this equates to approximately 375g – 525g in a 24-hour period.

CARBOHYDRATES DURING TRAINING

Scott Jurek is one of the most successful endurance runners the world has ever seen. His experience as an ultra-runner gives his running advice credibility above most others. The two formulae Scott suggests to use to work out your mid run carbohydrate consumption are:

- **Bodyweight in kilograms X 0.7 = grams of carbohydrates per hour**
- **Bodyweight in kilograms X 1.0 = grams of carbohydrates per hour**

For example if you weigh 70kg, you should aim to consume anywhere between 49 and 70g per hour. Knowing which of these formulae to use is dependent on a few factors, but the key reason to choose one over the other is down to the distance and intensity of your training run. Although your initial thought might be that the harder you run the more carbohydrate you'll need to consume to keep you going, it's actually the reverse – due to restricted blood flow the body is unable to assimilate and digest carbohydrate effectively. So, Scott's advice to work out how much carbohydrate you should be looking to consume on the run is as follows:

Consuming the lower-end formula (0.7g per kg of bodyweight)

- During training runs or races that require you to run at a reasonably high intensity, such as 85–90 per cent of maximum effort. Depending on your fitness levels, this can be sessions lasting anywhere from 90 minutes to up to three hours for a highly conditioned trail runner.
- As always, feel free to tweak levels if you find you need more carbohydrate towards the end of the session. Remember, however, that the digestive system struggles to digest carbohydrates at high intensities and you may find you get stomach cramps if your carbohydrate snack is too rich.

Consuming the higher-end formula (1.0 g per kg of bodyweight)

- During long-distance trail runs that require you to run at a steady pace of around 70–80 per cent of maximum effort.
- As there is more blood available for digestion, the body can tolerate and utilise higher levels of carbohydrate as the working muscles are not demanding so much blood to sustain your gentler running pace.

DO YOU NEED TO 'CARB UP' ON THE RUN?

Although many sports nutrition companies will lead you to believe that you should be consuming carbohydrate gels and snack bars on every training run, the truth is that unless you are running over a certain distance or for a certain length of time, snacking on carbohydrates is unnecessary. Your body has plenty of carbohydrate storage capacity to easily see you through a 90-minute run, so provided you have been vigilant with your carbohydrate consumption prior to training, unless you are planning to run further than 90 minutes, you do not need the extra carbohydrate.

CARBOHYDRATE SNACKS ON THE RUN

Working out how much carbohydrate you should consume on a longer run is one thing, but knowing what types of snack you should be eating is another. There are lots of different carbohydrate snacks available to runners, but, as always, you need to find what works for you. Often the decision comes down to personal taste preference and convenience of carrying the snacks with you while running. Try out a few options and see which ones you find convenient and tasty, and those best tolerated by your digestive system. Although some runners can tolerate all kinds of carbohydrate-rich snacks while on the run, others may find that sugar dense sports gels are too rich for their digestive systems and cause cramping and digestive discomfort. Find out early on what works for you and avoid copying what someone else uses – we're all different! Here are a few common snacks used by runners.

Table 10.1 Common carb snacks

Snack (weight/amount)	Approx. carbohydrate (g)
Bottle of Lucozade (250ml)	42
Mars bar (60g)	40
Banana (large)	30
Power bar (65g)	42
Carbohydrate gel (70g)	25

Whichever snack you choose, make sure you do not leave it too late to consume it or it might be too late for the carbohydrate to get into your bloodstream, thus rendering it ineffective.

THE GLYCAEMIC INDEX (GI)

The glycaemic index (GI) indicates how quickly your blood sugar levels rise when you eat a certain type of carbohydrate, placing each food in categories ranked 0–100. The faster the rise of glucose in our bloodstream after consuming a certain food type, the higher it is ranked on the glycaemic index, e.g. pure glucose is 100 on the scale, water is 0, and fresh vegetables rank low at around 40.

As always, there is much debate regarding whether runners should consume high or low GI food to maximise glycogen storage, but the opinion seems to be that in order to replenish stocks of carbohydrate most effectively, you should be looking to eat high GI carbs in the first six hours or so after training. High GI foods are also far preferable to consume during a run.

To give you an idea of which foods are classed as high, medium and low GI, take a look at table 10.2

which shows the glycaemic load, and estimates how much a particular food will raise a person's blood glucose level after eating. For example one unit of glycaemic load approximates the effect of consuming one gram of glucose.

Table 10.2

Food	Portion size	GI	Carbohydrate (g) per portion	GL per portion
High GI (> 70)				
Dates	6 (60 g)	103	40	42
Glucose	2 tsp (10 g)	99	10	10
French baguette	5 cm slice (30 g)	95	15	15
Lucozade	250 ml bottle	95	42	40
Baked potato	1 average (150 g)	85	30	26
Rice krispies	Small bowl (30 g)	82	26	22
Cornflakes	Small bowl (30 g)	81	26	21
Gatorade	250 ml bottle	78	15	12
Rice cakes	3 (25 g)	78	21	17
Chips	Average portion (150 g)	75	29	22
Shredded wheat	2 (45 g)	75	20	15
Bran flakes	Small bowl (30 g)	74	18	13
Cheerios	Small bowl (30 g)	74	20	15
Mashed potato	4 tbsp (150 g)	74	20	15
Weetabix	2 (40 g)	74	22	16
Bagel	1 (70 g)	72	35	25
Breakfast cereal bar (crunchy nut cornflakes)	1 bar (30 g)	72	26	19
Watermelon	1 slice (120 g)	72	6	4
Golden Grahams	Small bowl (30 g)	71	25	18
Millet	5 tablespoons (150 g)	71	36	25
Water biscuit	3 (25 g)	71	18	13
Wholemeal bread	1 slice (30 g)	71	13	9
Isostar	250 ml can	70	18	13
White bread	1 slice (30 g)	70	14	10

Food	Portion size	GI	Carbohydrate (g) per portion	GL per portion
Moderate GI (56–69)				
Fanta	262 ml	68	34	23
Sucrose	2 tsp (10 g)	68	10	7
Croissant	1 (57 g)	67	26	17
Instant porridge	250 g bowl	66	26	17
Cantaloupe melon	1 slice (120 g)	65	6	4
Couscous	5 tbsp (150 g)	65	35	23
Mars bar	1 bar (60 g)	65	40	26
Raisins	3 tbsp (60 g)	64	44	28
Rye crispbread	2 (25 g)	64	16	11
Shortbread	2 (25 g)	64	16	10
White rice	5 tbsp (150 g)	64	36	23
Tortillas/corn chips	1 bag (50 g)	63	26	17
Ice cream	1 scoop (50 g)	61	13	8
Muesli bar	1 bar (30 g)	61	21	13
Sweet potato	1 medium (150 g)	61	28	17
Pizza	1 slice (100 g)	60	35	21
Digestive biscuit	2 (25 g)	59	16	10
Pineapple	2 slices (120 g)	59	13	7
Basmati rice	5 tbsp (150 g)	58	38	22
Porridge	250 g bowl	58	22	13
Squash (diluted)	250 ml glass	58	29	17
Apricots	3 (120 g)	57	9	5
Pitta bread	1 small (30 g)	57	17	10
Power Bar	1 bar (65 g)	56	42	24
Sultanas	3 tbsp (60 g)	56	45	25
Rich tea biscuit	2 (25 g)	55	19	10
Potato – boiled	2 medium (150 g)	54	27	15
Oatmeal biscuit	2 (25 g)	54	17	9

Food	Portion size	GI	Carbohydrate (g) per portion	GL per portion
Low GI (< 55)				
Brown rice	5 tbsp (150 g)	55	33	18
Honey	1 tablespoon (25 g)	55	18	10
Muesli (Alpen)	1 small bowl (30 g)	55	19	10
Buckwheat	5 tbsp (150 g)	54	30	16
Crisps	1 large packet (50 g)	54	21	11
Sweetcorn	4 tbsp (150 g)	54	17	9
Kiwi fruit	3 (120 g)	53	12	6
Banana	1 (120 g)	52	24	12
Orange juice	1 large glass (250 ml)	52	23	12
Mango	½ (120 g)	51	17	8
Strawberry jam	1 tablespoon (30 g)	51	20	10
Rye bread	1 slice (30 g)	50	12	6
Muesli	1 small bowl (30 g)	49	20	10
Baked beans	1 small tin (150 g)	48	15	7
Bulgar wheat	5 tbsp (150 g)	48	26	12
Peas	2 tbsp (80 g)	48	7	3
Carrots	2 tbsp (80 g)	47	6	3
Macaroni	5 tbsp (180 g)	47	48	23
Grapes	Small bunch (120 g)	46	18	8
Pineapple juice	1 large glass (250 ml)	46	34	15
Sponge cake	1 slice (63 g)	46	36	17
Muffin, apple	1 (60 g)	44	29	13
Milk chocolate	1 bar (50 g)	43	28	12
All Bran	1 small bowl (30 g)	42	23	9
Orange	1 (120 g)	42	11	5
Peach	1 (120 g)	42	11	5
Apple juice	1 large glass (250 ml)	40	28	11

Food	Portion size	GI	Carbohydrate (g) per portion	GL per portion
Strawberries	21 (120 g)	40	3	1
Spaghetti	5 tbsp (180 g)	38	48	18
Plum	3 (120 g)	39	12	5
Apples	1 (120 g)	38	15	6
Pear	1 (120 g)	38	11	4
Protein bar	1 bar (80 g)	38	13	5
Tinned peaches – tinned in fruit juice	½ tin (120 g)	38	11	4
Yoghurt drink	1 glass (200 ml)	38	29	11
Plain yoghurt, low fat	1 large carton (200 g)	36	9	3
Custard	2 tbsp (100 g)	35	17	6
Chocolate milk	1 large glass (250 ml)	34	26	9
Fruit yoghurt, low fat	1 large carton (200 g)	33	31	10
Protein shake	1 carton (250 ml)	32	3	1
Skimmed milk	1 large glass (250 ml)	32	13	4
Apricot (dried)	5 (60 g)	31	28	9
Butter beans	4 tbsp (150 g)	31	20	6
Meal replacement bar	1 bar (40 g)	31	19	6
Lentils (green/ brown)	4 tbsp (150 g)	30	17	5
Chickpeas	4 tbsp (150 g)	28	30	8
Red kidney beans	4 tbsp (150 g)	28	25	7
Whole milk	1 large glass (250 ml)	27	12	3
Lentils (red)	4 tbsp (150 g)	26	18	5
Grapefruit	½ (120 g)	25	11	3
Cherries	Small handful (120 g)	22	12	3
Fructose	2 teaspoon (10 g)	19	10	2
Peanuts	Small handful (50 g)	14	6	1

Adapted with permission from Anita Bean's *The Complete Guide to Sports Nutrition*, 7th ed, 2013, Bloomsbury

CARBOHYDRATES BEFORE TRAINING

Post-training carbohydrate is most important, but a surprising number of recreational runners still believe that carb consumption on the morning or day of a run is the key to providing sufficient energy for a training run. It is a myth that consuming large quantities of carbohydrate on the morning of a run will greatly enhance your performance. The carbohydrates needed for training are more effective when consumed during the days leading up to a run, instead of a few hours before you leave. Whichever you believe is more important, it is crucial to get the timing of carbohydrate ingestion before a run right

Table 10.3 Good sources of carbohydrate

Food Source	Approx. carbohydrate (g)
Pasta	71 per 100g
Rice	30 per 100g
Potatoes	50 – average sized potato
Oats	48 per 80g
Bread	30g – 2 slices of toast

THE EARLY BIRD

Clearly, if you like to get your run in before the rest of the world has woken up, consuming a carbohydrate rich breakfast three hours before your run is simply not practical. Setting the alarm for a large bowl of porridge at 3 a.m. isn't conducive to anyone's lifestyle, except maybe professional athletes.

In these cases where you simply don't have the time to fit in a large breakfast, experimentation is often the best option you have to find out what foods suit your digestive system the best so close before setting off for a run. Everyone is different and different forms of carbohydrate in the early hours of the morning will vary from person to person. Popular choices for a 'quick and easy' breakfast which are often tolerated well by the digestive system include:

- A couple of pieces toast and honey
- Several pieces of fruit – such as a banana and/or apple or two
- Bagel with jam

Although these food choices work well with most runners and help to elevate blood sugar levels and get your muscles ready for training first thing in the morning, it is essential to remember that it is your carbohydrate consumption in the day(s) before training that will provide you with the energy needed to run on the trails. If you neglect your carbohydrates, then this breakfast will be far from sufficient to meet the energy demands of your trail run.

TIP – Carbohydrate-rich snack bars and gels are very handy for early morning runners to keep your glycogen (carbohydrate) levels up, so make sure you take a few with you and snack on one every 45 minutes or so during your run.

to ensure your blood sugar levels are spot on. Ideally, the best time to eat before a run is around **two to four hours** before your first step, but this varies from one person's digestive system to another.

Researchers at Loughborough University found that a level of 2.5g of carbohydrate per kg of body weight around three hours before exercise improved running endurance capacity by 9 per cent, clearly demonstrating the importance of your pre-run carbohydrate meal. So for you late-morning runners, a breakfast of porridge or muesli is a good choice and for mid-afternoon runners you can't go far wrong with a rice-based lunch.

CHALLENGING THE DOGMA

Five minutes on the Internet can pull up many different programmes or diets that contradict each other, even by as little as 0.1g. What works for one runner may not for another. However, recently there has been a major alternative school of thought which contradicts one of the most fundamental principles of sports nutrition, and it is fast gaining support.

With their book *The Art or Science of Low Carbohydrate Performance* (Beyond Obesity LLC, 2012), Jeff Volek PhD and Stephen Phinney PhD question the widely held belief that an endurance

>> Carbing up before training

runner's diet should contain a high percentage of carbohydrate. Their research has demonstrated that the human body can actually be encouraged to change its preference of carbohydrate as its primary fuel to fat – which is far more abundant in the body and arguably far more effective at providing energy for long-distance trail runs. They suggest that using fat rather than carbohydrate makes far more sense since:

- The human body can store (in the muscles and the liver) a maximum of just 2000cal worth of carbohydrate. This is enough to fuel approximately three hours of running or around 20 miles.
- Once our carbohydrate stores have been used up, we must find ways to replace the spent energy by consuming sugar-rich sports drinks or gels.
- The human body can store exceptionally large amounts of fat – upwards of 40,000cal worth, which Volek and Phinney say can be tapped into and used as energy for running.
- 40,000 calories is sufficient to keep us (hypothetically) running for 60 hours or in excess of 400 miles.

Based on this information, trail runners who have aspirations of racing in multiday events would be best served by tapping into their fat stores and unlocking them to provide the required energy to keep running and running, without needing to refuel on carbohydrate snacks, drinks and gels. Sounds great, right? Predictably, it's not that simple. Encouraging your body to change its fuel preference from carbohydrate to fat isn't simply a case of reducing your carbohydrate intake for a day or two and expecting your muscles to embrace fat as their source of energy – it's a bit more complicated than that.

CHANGE OF FUEL, CHANGE OF LIFESTYLE

The current received wisdom is that as exercise intensity increases, so does our reliance on carbohydrate as a source of energy. So, if we're sitting around doing nothing, the percentage of energy used to fuel our body comes predominantly from fat. However, as exercise intensity increases, from a walk, to a jog to a sprint, our reliance on carbohydrate to fuel movement increases proportionally, so that during an all-out sprint we are using 100 per cent carbohydrate as our energy source.

For years, we have accepted that as the intensity of training increases to around 65 per cent of VO_2 max, which is the same intensity as a decent paced jog, it is impossible for fat to be broken down fast enough to provide the energy needed to sustain exercise, hence the reason why a carbohydrate-rich diet has been long accepted to be the optimum dietary choice for the majority of competitive and recreational runners.

However, Volek and Phinney believe that provided you stick to a carefully controlled low-carbohydrate diet, it's possible to encourage your body to use its fat stores even at intensities higher than 65 per cent VO_2 – completely challenging a fundamental fact of endurance nutrition among mainstream sports scientists.

For you, as someone who has likely already spent many years running, either on the roads or the trails, this revelation and the challenge to conventional

belief might sound intriguing and worth exploring. Possibly it is, but there are two considerations which you must first think about. As appealing as the physical benefits might sound, do not underestimate the importance of your **biochemical individuality** and the impact such a dramatic change in eating habits can have on your general **lifestyle** outside of running.

Individuality

First and foremost, you are you – and you work differently to everyone else. Tests, research and proof can lead everyone to believe that a certain way of eating or training is the best way to do things, but no study ever (or very rarely) concludes that 100 per cent of the people they studied responded in exactly the same way to any given stimulus, nutrient or modality. Even Volek and Phinney, the proponents of the low-carbohydrate approach to endurance training, state that some people are better suited to a high carbohydrate diet. So my question is, if you are

BIOCHEMICAL INDIVIDUALITY

Roger Williams talks about how we're each built differently, and why this is important in terms of the food that we eat in his book *Biomechanical Individuality (Keats Publishing, 1998)*.

Study after study has shown that our organs vary greatly in size and shape, meaning the nutrients that drive them will also vary from one person to another. The overwhelming majority of sports nutrition books and articles will give us information on a one size fits all basis, so never forget that your organs and how they react to the food we eat vary enormously. One man's meat is another man's poison.

happy, healthy and perform well on a carbohydrate-rich diet, why change? If it ain't broke, don't fix it.

However, if you are not happy or feel there is room for improvement, you may very well benefit from changing the way you eat. If this is the case, I strongly suggest you read more into the subject of low-carbohydrate nutrition for endurance training.

Lifestyle

As intriguing as a low-carbohydrate diet might sound to help give your performance a boost on the trails, do not underestimate the dramatic effect that adopting such a diet will have on your life outside of running. As much as you enjoy trail running and wish to continue improving, if you also enjoy a good social life, such a diet can be incredibly difficult to adhere to and is even deemed by many to be anti-social.

The science behind the benefits of a low-carbohydrate diet is necessarily a bit complex, but in short it is based around the necessity to keep your insulin levels low. By suppressing insulin, i.e., eating a very low-carbohydrate diet, you give the body the ability to unlock its fat stores and use them for energy. However, just one sudden surge in insulin by consuming even the smallest amount of carbohydrate can disrupt this energy balance and make the body switch from using fat as energy back to carbohydrate. This means that to make a low-carbohydrate diet work for you and ensure you are burning fat while out on the trails, you must religiously limit your daily carbohydrate to around 50g – the same amount of carbs as are in two small apples. This means that the following foods are pretty much off limits... forever:

- Alcoholic drinks
- Most fruits
- Pasta
- Bread
- Potatoes
- Rice
- Crisps
- Chocolate
- Anything with sugar

Although it is possible to avoid these foods for long periods of time, it can be incredibly difficult in a world where carbohydrate-rich foods are everywhere.

At the end of the day, whether or not you choose to adopt, or look into adopting, this form of nutrition is up to you. It is controversial and certainly not suited to everyone, but I thought it was worth bringing to your attention so that you are aware that long-held nutritional beliefs can be, and indeed are, challenged in the search for optimum performance. Are such challenges justified? You may wish to find out for yourself, but if you do so, proceed cautiously.

PROTEIN – REBUILDING YOUR BODY

High quality protein is essential to ensure that tired and overworked muscles are given the correct nutrients to rebuild and repair themselves. Without daily adequate quantities or quality of dietary protein, the body is unable to meet muscular repair demands after running long distances on the trails. A consistent lack of protein can lead to a range of symptoms from affecting your endocrine system (which deals with the production of hormones) to an increased risk of injury as the body has been given inadequate building blocks to rebuild broken muscle tissue.

AMINO ACIDS

The body uses protein by breaking it down into individual building blocks commonly known as amino acids. Amino acids play a key role in virtually everything we do and provided there are sufficient amino acids available, predominantly obtained through the food we eat, the endurance runner's

body is able to function the way we expect it to: hormones and enzymes can be produced and sent to do their job, oxygen can be circulated around the body, energy can be produced and our temperature regulated, all of which is ultimately down to the availability of amino acids.

ESSENTIAL AND NON-ESSENTIAL AMINO ACIDS

We can get all the protein, and therefore amino acids, we need through our diet and the easiest way to ensure we're getting all of them is by consuming a carnivorous diet, including a range of meats, eggs and fish. These all contain what are known as **essential amino acids**, amino acids which cannot be manufactured by the body when it becomes

deficient in them. These types of proteins are called **complete proteins**.

In contrast, other foods such as vegetables, grains and beans, are classed as **incomplete proteins** and contain a range of non-essential and essential amino acids.

Mainstream advice to all athletes and endurance runners is to eat a balanced diet of varied protein-rich foods that contain complete and incomplete proteins, to ensure all amino acids are ingested and the body has all the building blocks at its disposal to repair and rebuild the body post-exercise and keep it functioning optimally. However, for religious or personal reasons, not all runners are willing to adhere to mainstream advice.

PROTEIN FOR VEGETARIAN AND VEGAN RUNNERS

If you are a non-meat eater, it is still possible to meet your body's amino acid requirements. Although common plant-based foods might only contain a selection of essential amino acids, combined they can meet all the protein demands of the body and you can be just as nutritionally balanced as a carnivorous runner.

HOW MUCH PROTEIN?

Although this question predictably attracts a mixture of views, the general advice is that runners should be aiming to consume between 1.2 and 1.4g of protein per kg of bodyweight. This would mean that a 70kg runner should be looking to consume 84–98g of protein/day. As a guide to how much this is in real terms, take a look Tables 10, 4 and 105.

TIMING YOUR PROTEIN INTAKE

The best time to eat your protein is immediately after training, where it can help maximise the storage of glycogen, and any time between training runs.

The important thing to remember is that as protein takes longer to digest than carbohydrate and it requires stomach acids to break it down, large amounts of protein are not recommended in the hours leading up to a training run. It's wise to leave a good three to four hours at least between a protein-rich meal and a training run. Having said that, protein replacements drinks are more digestible, so if you choose to drink them as part of your training diet, this timeframe may be a little more forgiving as the protein will be digested a lot faster as is therefore less likely to cause stomach complaints.

CARBOHYDRATE AND PROTEIN – MIXING IT UP

There is good evidence to suggest that by combining carbohydrate and protein in your post-

Table 10.4 Protein content in common foods (vegetarian)

Food Source	Approx. Protein (g)
Chick peas / 100g	8
Kidney beans / 100g	8
Tofu / 140g	11
Almonds – half a cup	16
Avocado – 450g	10
Quorn mince – 100g	12
Soy milk – 1 litre	15
Butter beans – 1 cup	12

Table 10.5 Protein content in common foods (non-vegetarian)

Food	Approx protein content (g)
Chicken breast – (2 small breasts)	30
Eggs (two medium)	18
Peanuts (a good handful)	24
Milk (1l)	35
Tuna – (a small drained tin)	24

run snack, you can actually enhance your body's ability to store away glycogen (carbohydrate) more effectively. According to a study at the University of Texas, when 112g of carbohydrate was combined

SCOTT JUREK – CHALLENGING BELIEFS

Winning an endurance event at any level is an incredible feat, but for Scott winning just one event was very much the start of an incredible career of competitive ultra-running. As a complete unknown, Scott took the lead in the famous Western States Endurance Run, a 100-mile event over the trails of the American Sierra Nevada range of mountains. He has since won this event not once, but seven times in a row, along with other races most trail runners could only dream of completing, let alone winning.

As incredible as his consistent victories have been, it is Scott's approach to endurance nutrition that has really got the trail-running community talking, since it challenges conventional belief of how to fuel the body for long-distance running.

Scott is a vegan and has been for years.

All of his wins and amazing feats of endurance have been fuelled by a plant-based diet, without a steak, chicken breast or fish fillet in sight. Conventional theory would have us believe that, as a vegetarian or vegan, it would be difficult to consume the essential amino acids necessary to rebuild the body after a high-mileage training run. Yet Scott's consistent success as a trail and ultra-runner proves that, for him at least, a plant-based diet is the optimal way to fuel his body and compete at the highest level.

If you want to find out more about Scott and what he has achieved, I strongly recommend his book *Eat and Run* (Bloomsbury, 2012).

---

with 40g of protein in a post-training drink it helped to increase the storage of glycogen by a massive 38 per cent when compared to consuming a drink with just carbohydrate. The most effective way to get this combination right straight after a run, is to use a blender at home and either prepare a milk-based drink when you get home after a run or take one with you if you are running/training elsewhere.

Mixing protein-rich foods such as nuts, seeds with milk and a banana are great choices for a tasty post-run drink and helps to replenish lost nutrients straight away.

For more substantial replenishment, your first meal after a long training run should be rich in both carbohydrate and protein. Good choices are pasta and tuna, spaghetti bolognaise or a jacket potato with a high protein filling such as tuna.

FATS – ARE THEY REALLY ALL THAT BAD?
FOCUS ON UNSATURATED FAT

Calorie-dense yet widely believed to be difficult to use in large quantities when running at intensities over 65 per cent of your maximum speed, large amounts of fat in your diet can hinder your performance. However, not all types of fat should be avoided. Unsaturated fats have been proven to be incredibly beneficial to the body whatever your activity levels but they are of particular importance to you as a trail runner.

The two types of unsaturated fats – mono-unsaturated and polyunsaturated – are both essential for our health:

OMEGA 3 AND 6

Omega 3 and 6 are essential fatty acids that cannot be made by the body, so it is vital you get them from your diet. Try to make a conscious effort to eat foods rich in unsaturated fat, especially Omega 3s such as oily fish, at least twice a week, to help keep your heart and joints healthy. Omega 6 fatty acids are actually found more abundantly in common foods such as eggs and avocado and nuts, so are much easier to consume.

The Omegas benefit the body in a variety of ways, from helping to keep joints lubricated and improving brain function to helping the body fight inflammation. The more research that goes into unlocking the properties and secrets of essential fatty acids such as Omega 3 and Omega 6, the more health benefits scientists seem to uncover.

COMMON OMEGA 3-RICH FOODS
- Salmon
- Mackerel
- Sardines
- Mussels
- Prawns
- Tuna steaks
- Flaxseed Oil
- Rapeseed Oil

KEY BENEFITS OF UNSATURATED FATTY ACIDS

Although research continues into the benefits of consuming unsaturated fatty acids, they provide a number of positive physiological effects to the endurance/trail runner. Studies have shown that Omega 3 fatty acids can lead to improvements in endurance thereby assisting long-distance runners in sustaining high levels of work for longer periods of time.

In addition, when you consider the following proven benefits of Omega 3 fatty acids, you'll see why they should feature regularly in your weekly eating plan:

- Improved delivery of oxygen and nutrients to the cells due to reduced blood viscosity
- More flexible red blood cell membranes and improved oxygen delivery
- Enhanced aerobic metabolism
- Increased energy levels and stamina
- Increased exercise duration and intensity
- Improved release of growth hormone in response to sleep and exercise, thereby improving recovery.

So next time you plan your weekly diet, make sure Omega 3 fatty acids feature no less than two to three times.

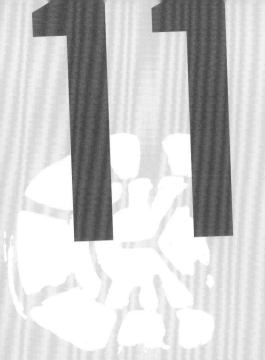

11

DRINKING FOR THE TRAILS

On the basis that humans are made up of around 70 per cent water, it makes logical sense that as endurance runners we should be particularly vigilant of how well we hydrate our cells before, during and after training. When you consider that a 10 per cent drop in hydration status is enough to stop us from training and a 20 per cent drop is enough to kill us, being aware of how well-hydrated you are before, during and after a long run is essential if you want to get the most out of your training and build your fitness safely.

As important as hydration is, however, in recent years there have sadly been plenty of cases worldwide where the message has been taken too seriously, resulting (sometimes fatally) in cases of runners becoming over-hydrated. It's always the case that 'a little knowledge can be a dangerous thing' and this is certainly the case when it comes to hydrating the body for a run – particularly long trail runs in the heat. To make matters even more confusing, like the 'carbohydrate vs. fat for fuelling your training runs' debate (*see* pages 166–9), in recent years there is also a debate rumbling among exercise scientists that as a collective group, runners obsess far too much over the benefits and necessity of taking on fluids regularly during training. Do we overdramatise the risks or are we justified in setting

off for long runs with hydration packs and water bottles?

OVERWATERED?
DETERMINING HYDRATION STATUS

Outside the laboratory, finding out how well hydrated you are is actually very easy. Although the following test is a little crude (in more ways than one), it is commonly used by many amateur sports people who need a quick way to check their hydration status. Looking closely at the colour of your urine might not be the most dignified part of trail running, but the colour of the stream can tell you quite a lot about how well hydrated your body is and whether you are 'good to go' for a long trail run with the confidence that you are at least

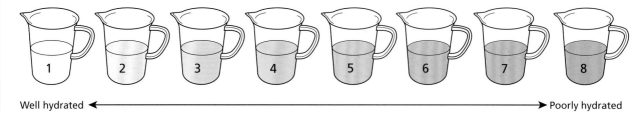

Well hydrated ←   → Poorly hydrated

>> **Figure 11.1 Urine colour guide to dehydration**

starting well hydrated. Figure 11.1 is a guide to testing your level of hydration next time you take to the trails. As a general rule, the clearer your urine is, the better hydrated you are. Therefore, before you set out for a run of any notable distance, you should be looking to pass urine well into the well hydrated colour. If you start out mid-range, there is a chance your performance could be affected as your body becomes even further dehydrated during your exertions on the trail.

CALCULATING YOUR INDIVIDUAL RATE OF FLUID LOSS

The rate at which the human body loses fluid at rest and during a run varies from person to person. If you train with a friend or a group of people it's likely you would have noticed that during a training session your rate of perspiration will vary greatly from others' – some may sweat more or less than you, despite the fact you're all running at the same intensity. As a result, it is essential you find out early on in your trail-running training how much fluid

HYDRATION FACTS
Did you know...?

- If you squeezed every drop of water out of an average man, you'd end up with around 45l (80 pints).
- The more dehydrated you become, the less able your body is to sweat.
- Every 1000ml of sweat that evaporates from your body results in a loss of approx 600kcals of heat energy.
- A two-hour trail run in moderately warm conditions could lead to sweat loss of 3–4l.
- During exercise, your leg muscles produce up to 500ml of water every two to three hours.

you lose during a run so that you can take steps to reduce a significant drop in hydration status that will affect performance and possibly your health.

The easiest way to give you an idea of your fluid loss during a run is by simply using a set of bathroom scales.

THE BATHROOM SCALES DEHYDRATION TEST

Just before you're about to get ready for your run and head out of the door, step on your bathroom

B VITAMIN CONFUSION

If you take vitamins or you plan to for your upcoming training, be aware that vitamin B_2 (riboflavin) causes your urine to turn yellow a few hours after you have taken it. This is not a sign of severe dehydration, but is simply the body expelling the excess riboflavin through your urine.

scales (preferably naked) and jot down your exact weight. Then get dressed, head out for your trail run, which ideally should be around one hour to give you a good idea of your hourly fluid loss rate, and, crucially, do not take on any fluid before, during or after your run.

As soon as you return, before you visit the bathroom or rehydrate, step back on the scales (again naked) and mark down your weight again.

Although some of your weight loss will have come from lost glycogen and fat stores, the majority will be as a result of fluid loss through respiration and sweat. As a rough indicator, 1 pint (560ml) equals 1lb (450g), so a recorded weight loss of 3lbs would indicate you have lost somewhere in the region of 3 pints (just over 1.5l) of sweat during your exertions on the trail. You'd therefore need to replenish your fluids with a similar amount post run.

You'll get a good idea how accurate this test is by rehydrating with the same quantity of fluid you have theoretically lost and if the urine test gives you a clear or pale colour after drinking this quantity, you'll know that the calculation is accurate.

Be aware, however, that your rate of fluid loss during your run will vary enormously depending on the length and intensity of your run, ambient temperature and humidity of the atmosphere. By writing down your rate of fluid loss after runs of varying length, intensity and climate, you will be far better placed to know how much fluid you should be taking on during your race, whatever the conditions. To ensure this test is as accurate as possible, try the following tips:

- By weighing yourself naked, you'll ensure you don't get an inaccurate reading from mud or sweat-soaked clothes
- Always use the same scales in the same location to ensure accurate readings.
- Perform the test before/after a run in a variety of conditions – long, short, hilly, fast, intense, etc.
- Make a diary of your post run weight loss.
- If you drink fluid during a run, take how much you have drunk into account when you weigh yourself after the run.
- On race day or long run days, find out the expected conditions and refer back to your diary to see how much fluid you can expect to lose by comparing it to previous training runs in similar conditions.

DEHYDRATION AND PERFORMANCE

We've touched on the fact that the perils of dehydration are sometimes over-exaggerated, but that certainly doesn't mean you should ever take on a long trail in a dehydrated state, or forget to take fluid along with you. During a long run where your sweat loss can easily exceed 1l an hour, as capable as your body is of adapting to dehydration by secreting an anti-diuretic hormone, the loss of fluid from your body can still have a detrimental effect on your performance. Just a 2 per cent reduction in your weight as a result of dehydration can lead to a drop in your ability to maintain aerobic exercise. It has been proven that the human body can lose up to 10–20 per cent of its maximal aerobic capacity

AVERAGE JOE

Studies referenced by William Costill and Jack Wilmore in *Physiology of Sport and Exercise*, (Human Kinetics, 2012) indicate that a 70kg runner will metabolise around 245g (8oz) of carbohydrate and lose as much as 1500ml of fluid during a one-hour run, with this figure rising in warm conditions. This fluid and carbohydrate loss can equate to a weight loss of as much as 4lbs (2kg).

> ## THE DANGERS OF DEHYDRATION
> If your body becomes dehydrated then your blood becomes less viscous, making it harder for the heart to transport it around the body. This causes the heart rate to increase and can result in premature fatigue. Dehydration also makes it harder for the body to regulate its internal temperature.

when this small drop in hydration is experienced, so, fluid replacement during long runs is vital if you want to maintain performance.

Other physiological functions that are affected by dehydration include:

- Decreased concentration and alertness
- Reduced rate of sweating
- Increase in body temperature
- Reduced blood volume
- Reduced strength

BLOOD IS THICKER THAN WATER

Around 80 per cent of blood is water. Even if you begin a long run in a well-hydrated state it doesn't take long before your fluid loss through sweat and breath evaporation reaches litres rather than millilitres, especially if your running intensity is high and the conditions are warm. During a long run, as you continue to sweat, the water content of your blood will gradually begin to reduce, causing a raft of physiological changes within the body.

As your blood loses water from prolonged sweating, the heart is made to work harder to pump thicker blood through your arteries to the working muscles. This increases your working heart rate and leads to premature fatigue. By replacing lost fluids throughout your run, you can help prevent or at least reduce the rate of water loss from the blood, thereby helping to reduce fatigue and a drop in performance.

SPORTS DRINK VS. WATER

It seems you can't watch a televised sporting event, open a magazine or pass a bus stop without seeing some form of advertising of the energy-giving and performance-enhancing benefits of sports drinks. Aside from this aggressive marketing campaign, the jury is actually still out in the scientific community as to whether sports drinks such as Lucozade, Powerade and Gatorade can actually enhance performance. As a trail runner, who will be negotiating miles and miles of steep and complex trails, should your water bottles or hydration packs be filled with sugar-rich sports drink or good old-fashioned water? The answer is all down to run intensity, length and ultimately your rate of sweat loss.

In short, the longer and/or more intense your trail run, the more likely the physiological need for a glucose-rich sports drink. Isotonic sports drinks, the ones most commonly used and marketed to both serious and recreational runners contain around 7–10 per cent glucose, which, according to many experts, is the ideal concentration of sugar to maximise rehydration and maintain optimal blood sugar levels for performance.

As a rough guide, use the following categories of training runs to give you an idea of when sports drinks are necessary:

NICE AND EASY TRAIL RUN: WATER WILL SUFFICE

For easy, relatively flat runs lasting less than an hour, sports drinks cannot really offer you much more than water. Although not harmful, they certainly will not give you the energy boosting impetus that the advertisers so desperately want you to buy into.

HARD AND FAST TRAIL RUNS: SPORTS DRINKS CAN HELP

For high intensity runs lasting up to 60 minutes, there is a good argument for the use of sports drinks as they may well give you an advantage over the course of the session. They may not be vital, but there is evidence to suggest that their ingestion may be beneficial to some.

SPORTS DRINKS TIPS

- Everyone reacts differently to sports drinks and it's not uncommon to experience abdominal cramps when you first use them, so always test them out during rest rather than for the first time during a long run.
- Experiment with different brands to find a flavour you like and one which suits your digestive system.
- Hypertonic sports drinks (higher in sugar) are best consumed after a run due to their high sugar content preventing absorption in the stomach. Post-exercise, the high sugar content can be more easily absorbed and help to replenish your internal carbohydrate stores.
- Make your own isotonic drink by simply mixing 250ml of water with 250ml of fruit juice, or adding 20–40g of sugar to every 500ml of water. Add a pinch of salt to the mix to increase electrolyte levels. These drinks are so important because they replace salts and sugars which are used up and sweated out during exercise.

LONG AND SLOW TRAIL RUN: SPORTS DRINK SHOULD FEATURE

When your trail runs last longer than 60 minutes, there is an extremely good argument to take sports drinks with you. Although water alone will help and is certainly required over the course of a long run, the electrolyte (salt) and sugar content of sports drinks help to replace salts lost through sweat and sugars expended through your running efforts. As a general rule, rehydrate with a bottle of sports drink (500ml) every hour while out on long runs lasting over an hour.

DRINKING BEFORE A RUN

Getting your fluids right before you head off for a run is fairly easy. In the hours leading up to your run, drink regularly – though not excessively – and use the urine test every time you need the bathroom. When you notice your urine is running clear or it's pale straw-coloured, you know you are well hydrated and there is no need to continue taking on additional fluid.

As a rough guide you should be looking to take on around 500ml of fluid a couple of hours before you hit the trails. As practical as this advice might be, it's not particularly helpful if your planned trail run is scheduled for dawn. In this instance, it's best to consume a slightly smaller volume of fluid before you set off and ensure you take at least 500–1000ml of water or preferably sports drink with you in your water bottle or hydration pack.

DRINKING ON THE RUN

The timing of your fluid intake during a run is far more important than you might think. The tendency of many runners is to simply drink when they are thirsty, but this is likely to be far too late to help maximise your hydration status during a long trail run. When out running the trails it's generally recommended you drink small amounts regularly from as early as

15 minutes into a long run. This ensures your body is able to use the fluid it is taking in, and if you are consuming a drink containing carbohydrate, it also ensures maximal fluid absorption and helps to keep blood sugar levels normal.

The exact amount of fluid you should be drinking on any given run is an area (as always) of much debate among exercise scientists.

Due to the variances of our metabolisms, physiques, body compositions, gender, training intensities, etc., coming up with an accurate number of recommended litres per hour is not only impossible to state with any great deal of accuracy but also pretty confusing. However, to give you a guideline to start off with – bearing in mind that you are responsible for adapting this to suit your rate of fluid loss – you should be looking to consume anywhere between **150 and 300ml of fluid every 20 minutes** that you are running. You should be looking towards the higher end of this if the conditions are warm, you're a heavy runner or the intensity/speed of your session is high.

DRINKING AFTER A RUN

However far your trail run has taken you, rehydrating soon after you've finished is essential. When you consider there's every chance you've just lost a good litre or two of water from your blood and muscles, it needs to be replaced so that your body can function optimally. Forgetting to replace fluids after a run and remaining in a dehydrated state for the rest of the day can lead to a range of issues including:

- Headaches
- Nausea
- Dizziness
- Muscle cramps
- Overwhelming tiredness
- Lethargy

It is actually quite easy to guess how much fluid you need to consume post run. First, there is the good old urine test (*see* page 176). Simply drink small amounts regularly soon after your run and stop when your urine is back to being clear or a pale straw colour.

Another way to gauge fluid loss is to consider the time spent exercising and the temperature you were in. As mentioned previously the rule of thumb is that you lose approximately 1–2l of fluid per hour during a moderately paced trail run, so despite taking on fluids during the run you should be looking to rehydrate with a similar volume in the hours of recovery following the session.

There is no need to get too precise about quantity. Provided your wee is back to normal and running clear within a few hours of finishing your run, consider yourself rehydrated.

HYPERNATREMIA

This chapter began by questioning whether there was a need to consume water at all during exercise, then went on to argue that on balance, yes there is, and now I'm going to finish by warning you of the risks of drinking too much water.

Overhydration (or water toxicity) can be far more serious than the risks of dehydration and for trail runners taking on long, complex and challenging trail routes in the summer, the risk, although low, is very real if you are not aware of the dangers of overhydration.

>> *Take on fluids as soon as you've finished*

LEACHING ELECTROLYTES

One of the key ingredients in our blood is **electrolytes** (salts). Without the right balance of salts or even a deficiency, our cells are unable to regulate their water content, which can lead to a condition known as hyponatremia.

Although we usually consume sufficient quantities of salts to ensure this balance remains normal, an imbalance can be created if we consume excessive quantities of water and combine it with an excessive amount of sweating. By over-compensating with our water intake in preparation for a long run in warm conditions, a situation can occur where we dilute the electrolyte content of the blood. When you combine this with an increased rate of sweat loss, where we lose salts through our sweat, it can easily lead to a deficiency in blood electrolyte levels and severe ill health.

READ THE SIGNS: HYPONATREMIA

Common symptoms of hyponatremia include:

- Dizziness
- Headaches
- Muscle cramps
- Nausea
- Tiredness
- Weakness
- Confusion
- Lack of consciousness

If you or a fellow runner are suffering from any of these symptoms, it is vital you seek medical help immediately. Hyponatremia can be an incredibly serious condition if not treated quickly, so be aware of it and take appropriate action if you think hyponatremia is likely.

However, diagnosing an ill runner with hyponatraemia is incredibly difficult to do – even if you have a medical background. As the symptoms are very similar to dehydration and hypoglycaemia, making a confident diagnosis without knowing the runner's fluid consumption (or lack of it) is nearly impossible.

If you see a runner who you suspect might be hyponatraemic, first and foremost call for medical assistance and tell them what you suspect the problem might be. In the meantime, if you can encourage the ill runner to take on anything salty such as an electrolyte sports drink, it will help replace lost salts before the medical backup arrives and administers a saline drip.

HOW MUCH IS TOO MUCH?

It is impossible to say how much water you would have to consume and how much you would have to sweat to suffer from hyponatremia, as it depends on your electrolyte levels in the first place. However, provided you follow all of the advice contained within this chapter, the chances of you suffering from hyponatremia are incredibly low.

12 COMMON TRAIL INJURIES: DIAGNOSIS AND TREATMENT

"There are two types of runners – those who are injured and those who are about to get injured."

Popular runners' phrase

As disheartening and defeatist as this might sound, sadly there is a degree of truth in the above saying. Despite the fact that trail paths are far softer underfoot than most road surfaces, thereby reducing impact forces to the lower back, the uneven and unpredictable nature of the trails present a very different range of injury risk.

Very few things on a trail route remain consistent from one run to the next, so developing a respect for the trail and avoiding complacency is the first thing you need to do if you plan to avoid picking up injuries. Protruding rocks and roots have a nasty habit of appearing out of nowhere, so be vigilant and respectful of the potential hazards.

In Chapter 3, I explained the importance of keeping your body well conditioned by ensuring your proprioception and lower leg strength are all trained regularly, so that you can help prevent injury by becoming a more balanced and agile runner.

Whereas the importance of these off-road exercises cannot be underestimated, at the same time it is a little unrealistic and inaccurate to suggest that developing an incredibly balanced, agile and strong lower leg musculature and core will make you immune to all possible injuries. You can develop a Herculean core and balance enough to run on a tightrope, but the trail can still get the better of you when you least expect it.

At the end of the day, you are going to have to accept that some injuries are almost impossible to avoid and have to be put down to simple bad luck. Ankle sprains, muscle pulls and shin splints are all common injuries and can strike with varying degrees of severity.

In this chapter we'll look at a selection of common injuries, including how to diagnose and best treat them, so that you can get back up on your feet and hit the trails again.

>> Trail paths can be unpredictable

SOFT TISSUE INJURIES

The overwhelming majority of the injuries you are likely to sustain while trail running will be to the soft tissue structures of the body, specifically the lower leg. Soft tissues of the body include ligaments, tendons and muscles and are particularly at risk from injury when joints or limbs change direction or speed suddenly and tension in the soft tissue becomes too great. This tension can cause small or even large numbers of muscle, tendon or ligament fibres to tear, creating a significant amount of discomfort and potentially weeks of rehabilitation.

THE GOOD NEWS

Amid the pain, the swelling, the inability to walk and the possible weeks off the trails, there is a bit of good news when it comes to picking up a soft tissue injury. Treatment in the overwhelming majority of cases is very straightforward and the speed at which the injury heals and is strong enough again to hit the trails is ultimately dependent on one person – you. Physiotherapists and physical therapists can of course play a significant role in giving the injury a helping healing hand by using techniques such as ultrasound, but you are in control of your own destiny; you have a major influence over how long it takes for your injury to heal, particularly in the early stages. You can easily shave weeks from your time spent convalescing by complying with the suggested treatment protocols. Sadly, compliance to medical advice is something, in my experience, which most runners are not particularly good at – which can be bad news for your injury.

THE BAD NEWS

Incurring an injury at any time during training is frustrating, but when you pick one up in the middle of a rigorous training regime and you're told to rest up for a few weeks, common sense often flies out of the window and you begin making poor decisions in an effort to get back to your training schedule. Let's be honest: runners are stubborn. As a runner for over two decades, on both road and trail, I know this all too well. Although there's an argument that those in glass houses shouldn't throw stones, when it comes to injuries I have (mostly) fought my instinct to carry on through the pain and give my injuries the necessary time to rest and recover.

But as a fitness professional and sports therapist, I have seen hundreds of runners make their injuries infinitely worse by running through pain. Avoid this at all costs – it will make things worse in the long-run.

THE THREE MOST COMMON SOFT TISSUE INJURIES

With over 30 separate muscles in the lower leg alone, there are dozens of potential muscles whose fibres are at risk of tearing if you take a sudden twist or trip on a trail route. Add to that the large muscles of the upper leg which help to power you over the trails and the potential for soft tissue damage of the muscles alone is significant. When you also factor in the tendons and ligaments, narrowing the injuries down to the three most common is not easy! However, due to the vulnerability of certain muscles,

INJURY CASE STUDY

I once had a client who was in training for a trail race and was showing encouraging signs that all the training protocols we implemented into his regime were working really well. As someone who had only taken up trail running in the past six months, he was showing great promise and, above all, thorough enjoyment from his training.

However, courtesy of a large tree root hidden under fallen autumnal leaves, he went over on his ankle and damaged ligaments and tendons. After initial adherence to the treatment procedure, he struggled to grasp the concept that rest and a complete break from running was the best option, and not four weeks later he was running/walking (and ultimately hobbling) up scenic trail routes in Scotland.

For what should have been a six-to-eight-week period of good rehab and rest, it took over 12 months for the client to finally become pain-free and fully able to confidently hit the trails again. Although this is an extreme example, it clearly demonstrates that not only can a premature return to training after an injury make your injury worse, but it can significantly delay the time it takes to recover from the injury.

tendons and ligaments and the pressure they face on the trails, there are three injuries which tend to crop up more frequently than others:

1. Ankle sprain
2. Achilles tendonitis
3. Shin Splints

ANKLE SPRAIN

Perhaps the most common injury trail runners can pick up is a twisted ankle. Spraining ankle ligaments is so easily done when traversing challenging trail paths that it's likely you'll experience an ankle sprain of some degree during your trail-running career.

Although there are several different types of ankle sprain, dependent on what angle you go over on your ankle, the treatment and prognosis are similar for all and, unfortunately, recovery time can sometimes be frustratingly long.

Injury snap shot
The two ankle ligaments you're likely to sprain are sited on the lateral side (outside) of your foot and

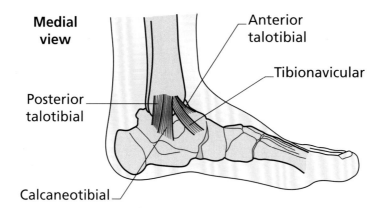

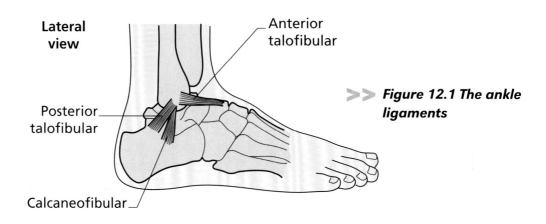

>> **Figure 12.1 The ankle ligaments**

are the calcaneofibular ligament and the anterior talofibular ligament. Of these two, it is the latter that is most often torn. Although you can sprain ligaments on the medial side (inside) of the foot, these are far less commonly injured during trail running. Due to the forward momentum that trail runners generate while out training – on the flat let alone running downhill – all it takes is for the surface beneath to suddenly become rocky and uneven and in a matter of milliseconds the ankle joint can lose its stability. When you combine that lack of stability with the forward momentum of the body, the stabilising ligaments in the ankle are exposed to the risk of being over-stretched and rupturing.

Diagnosis

Diagnosing an ankle sprain is often easily done even without a medical background; however, in extreme cases where there is significant pain and swelling, you should assess the ankle isn't broken.

In most cases, ankle sprains out on the trails are minor and low grade ligament sprains. Although painful, the long-term health of the ankle joint is not affected and with good treatment and rest, running can be resumed in a matter of weeks.

Common signs that you have picked up an inversion sprain, i.e., an injury to either the calcaneofibular or anterior talofibular ligament, include:

- sudden shooting pain on the outside of the ankle, often just in front of the outer ankle bone;
- pain when you stand on your foot and when you wiggle the foot around; and
- swelling around the outer ankle bone.

Plan of action

On the basis that by far the most common place you'll suffer an ankle sprain is out on the trails, possibly many miles from help, it is essential you

KEEP ON MOVING

Just because you have a sprained ankle it doesn't mean you need rest completely. Although reducing the swelling and bruising is key in the early stages, gentle mobility exercises for the joint are recommended to help prevent the joint from seizing up. Basic ankle movements, such as pointing your toes and then raising them, can help to encourage the synovial fluid in the joints to keep the joint mobile and functional (*see* page 94).

Taking it a step further, just because you can't run it doesn't mean you can't maintain a decent level of cardiovascular fitness via swimming, indoor rowing or cycling, all of which take the weight off your ankle. Provided the exercise does not initiate pain, there are plenty of ways to keep your heart pumping while your ankle repairs itself.

have medical supplies with you and some form of communication, such as a mobile phone.

In the early stages of the injury, especially if the sprain is severe, it's likely you'll have to loosen your shoe or even remove it completely to ease discomfort from swelling, so there should be a bandage or tubing in your bag to compress the ankle immediately.

If you are able to walk, then do so carefully, remembering that as the integrity of the ankle joint has been compromised, it is now far less stable and unable to balance on rough terrain. If you can, find a branch or two to use as a walking stick is incredibly useful in helping take the pressure off the ankle. If you have a mobile signal, call for help and try to get someone to come and help you off the trail. If your sprain is severe and the swelling and pain worsen,

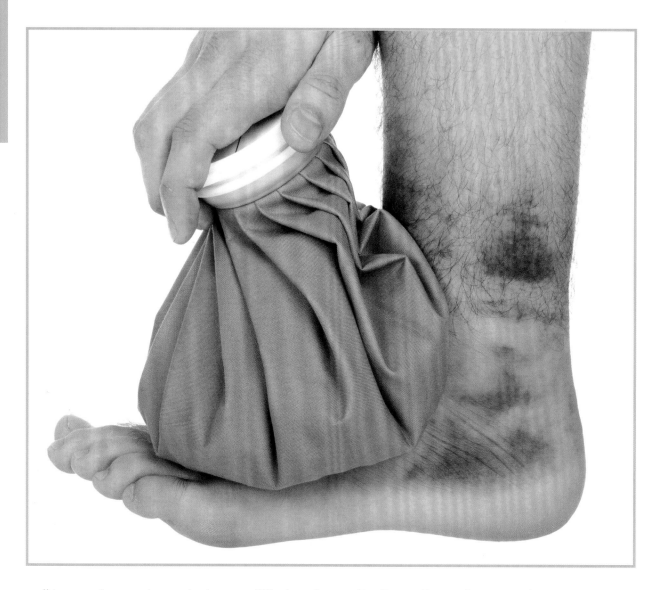

walking may become increasingly more difficult and you'll need help to get you to safety.

Treatment

Short term: The treatment for an inversion sprain is often very straightforward. Although treatment can get complicated if tendons of the certain lower leg muscle have also been damaged, provided it is just the ankle ligaments which have been affected, the RICE protocol is your first mode of treatment.

- **R = Rest** – Do not be tempted to go out running anytime soon. Rest your ankle and give it time to repair itself.
- **I = Ice** – By applying ice to the injured ankle you can significantly reduce the swelling and inflammation in a matter of days, so try to apply ice several times a day.
- **C = Compression** – By compressing the ankle joint you can help to reduce swelling and bleeding.

- **E = Elevation** – By elevating the ankle above the heart, you can reduce the blood flow to the ligaments in the early stages of injury, thereby helping to reduce swelling and bleeding.

Long term: After a few days, provided you have adhered to the RICE protocol, you will notice a significant reduction in both swelling and pain. When these have both gone, you can then move on to more advanced rehabilitation exercises that increase the range of movement and test balance on your injured ankle to help improve your proprioception (see p.57).

ACHILLES TENDONITIS

Unlike an ankle sprain, Achilles tendonitis is an injury which gradually creeps up on you (unless you've completely ruptured it, of course).

The Achilles tendon is a long, fibrous tendon that originates from the calf muscle and inserts onto your heel bone (calcaneus). It is an extremely strong tendon and is worked incredibly hard whenever you hit the trails.

As a trail runner encountering rugged and changeable terrain, you must be vigilant in the care of your Achilles tendons. Ensure you follow all necessary stretching and warm-up protocols before your run to reduce your chances of irritating your Achilles and initiating an inflammatory response.

Injury snap shot

Due to the work and load that the Achilles tendon is asked to endure for hours on end, the risk of injury is significant. What might also make for uncomfortable reading for some of you is that after the age of 25, the Achilles tendon begins to show signs of degenerative change. However, this does not mean that tendonitis is inevitable – far from it.

Despite the demands you place on your Achilles, they are ultimately designed to be incredibly tough and tolerate long periods of activity. Although trail

> ### ACHILLES CONDITIONS
> Although Achilles tendonitis might be the best known and perhaps most common injury afflicting the Achilles tendon, there are several other medical terms and conditions for pain in and around this part of the lower leg. Achilles peritendonitis, tendonosis and tenosynovitis all sound confusing but they are simply a diagnosis of the different layers/area of the tendon that are inflamed. Be sure to seek medical advice to ensure you are treating the correct condition.

running in itself is unlikely to cause them to become inflamed and problematic, other factors such as poor choice of footwear and sudden changes in training intensity may very well contribute to a gradual inflammatory response. As with any injury, prevention is far better than cure and this is especially the case with Achilles tendonitis.

To make sure you do everything you can to look after your Achilles tendons and to dramatically reduce your chances of contracting Achilles tendonitis, take a look at the three-point checklist below:

1. A certain amount of pronation – inward rolling of the foot – is perfectly normal during a running gait, however if the inward rolling is excessive it can lead to injuries to the foot, Achilles tendons and knees. If you have excessive pronation when you run, make sure you choose trail shoes which help to correct it. Although the softer trail surface is more forgiving than the road in this respect, if you are a severe over-pronator, it's worth getting the right shoes or in-soles to prevent aggravating your Achilles.

OVER-PRONATION AND TRAILS

If you have come from the world of road running, you'll probably be all too familiar with the term over-pronation and how it can affect your choice of running shoe. In short, the term over-pronation refers to an excessive inward rolling of the foot when you progress through gait from heel strike to taking off again from the forefoot. If you over-pronate as a road runner, it can be picked up via a gait analysis and advice will be offered as to which type of supportive shoe you should wear to minimise this excessive inward rolling and thereby reduce your chances of injury.

When you make the transition to the trails however, many runners are surprised at the lack of trail shoes available for over-pronators. The vast majority of trail shoes offer neutral support and only a handful of trail shoes on the market are manufactured to correct runners who over-pronate. The obvious question to this is why?

Leading trail-running shoe manufacture Brooks, whose Cascadia Trail shoe was designed with the help of trail-running legend Scott Jurek, give their explanation of why trail shoes generally do not offer support for over-pronators:

"Unlike running on road conditions where the surface underfoot tends to be consistently even, allowing us to guide the foot in a certain way with fixed components in the shoe, running on trails involves terrain that is inherently unstable and changeable, causing the body to adjust its balance constantly. In order to compensate for the destabilising effect of the terrain the body needs to use its own proprioceptive senses and have full control over the movement of each foot with each stride. To this end we do not incorporate stabilising components in trail shoes, such as we might in a road shoe, as the aim is never to interfere with the body's movement but to encourage it in an optimal fashion. On rougher terrain this means facilitating the body's ability to respond to changing conditions underfoot by allowing the feet freedom of movement so that the body can adjust the direction of movement as and when the ground requires."

2. Avoid increasing the intensity of your trail runs too quickly. This includes adding in excessive numbers of inclines, excessive time spent on the trails and running too regularly.

3. Stretch your calf muscles regularly, particularly if you find that they are often very tight (*see* page 102 for suggested calf stretches). Reducing muscle stiffness ensures the Achilles tendons are not placed under excessive strain while out running.

Diagnosis

The gradual onset of Achilles tendonitis often makes diagnosis in the early stages very difficult. In addition, there are a selection of other injuries which involve the Achilles tendon, so accurate diagnosis can be tricky. However, the key signs to look for are:

- stiffness in the Achilles tendon first thing in the morning – especially when trying to stand on tip-toe;
- stiffness and mild discomfort before and after training; and
- significant discomfort on palpating a certain point on the Achilles tendon. You may also notice a little bit of swelling.

Treatment

Like most soft tissue injuries, when you start showing the early signs of pain and inflammation ice is your best friend. The key for treating Achilles tendonitis or any other form of Achilles pain successfully is to catch it early and not soldier on through pain in the hope that it will get better. Once it's inflamed, running will only make the inflammation worse and the more you run, not only will it gradually become more painful but it will also increase the length of time it takes to recover from the injury. In some cases it can take many months to recover from Achilles tendonitis, so my advice is to get the injury looked at by a specialist as soon as possible so that you can have the best advice for your particular injury and its severity.

SHIN SPLINTS

Shin splints are a very common injury in runners and can be incredibly frustrating to treat. Anyone is susceptible to them, but it is often those new to running and the trails who are most likely to suffer. To make matters worse, there are different types of shin splints, all of which are caused by different factors and have subtle differences in the way they are best treated.

For trail runners, by far the most common form of shin splint can be felt on the muscle at the front of the shin or on the inside.

Injury snap shot

Shin pain and discomfort both during and after a training run is most commonly called shin splints. The location, cause and severity of the shin pain are the three key factors which need to be determined if a successful diagnosis and treatment programme are to be formulated.

Shin splints can strike at any time, regardless of how experienced you are on the trails. Although the cause is varied, shin splints are often initiated by

extrinsic factors such as a sudden change in training intensity or even dramatic change in the type of trail surface on which you are running. Although you might feel your heart and lungs can easily cope with the change of intensity and more challenging underfoot conditions, the network of muscles in your lower legs might suffer. For example, a simple shift from a gravel trail to a bridle path has the potential to interfere with your lower leg biomechanics and place unfamiliar demands on the lower leg muscles.

Diagnosis

Due to the number of different types of shin splints you can contract, diagnosing the exact type can be difficult, so official diagnosis is best left to a professional. However, if you experience any of the following, it's likely you have a form of shin splint:

- Tenderness of the muscles next to your shin bone
- Lower leg pain eases during rest but returns when running resumes
- Swelling in certain areas of the lower leg
- Pain when you point your toes or flex your foot
- Foot numbness
- Muscle weakness in your main shin muscle called the tibilas anterior

Treatment

Often the best treatment for shin splints of any kind is to rest for a few days and reduce the inflammation by applying ice to the affect area of tenderness while taking anti-inflammatory medication **if recommended by your health care professional.**

If pain continues after treatment, it's possible the shin splints could be caused by some biomechanical issues such as short and/or weak muscles. Incorrect footwear may also be to blame, so if problems persist I'd strongly recommend seeking advice from a qualified health professional.

SKIN INJURIES

Long runs on challenging surfaces not only expose your soft tissues to the risk of injury, but skin injuries such as blisters and abrasions from falls on to rocks or even foliage are very common for trail runners of all abilities.

BLISTERS

As common as they are annoying, you will no doubt at some point develop a blister somewhere on your foot or toe(s). If you have been lucky to avoid them when road running, I'm afraid that due to the nature of the terrain underfoot and the regularity of foot movement within your shoe, there's a good chance your luck will run out on the trail.

Caused by the rubbing together of two layers of skin, poor quality socks or even badly fitted shoes, as well as the combination of heat and moisture, blisters slowly swell full of fluid, causing pressure and pain at the site of the affliction. If left untreated and uncovered, blisters have the potential to cause misery as they will continue to get more painful the longer you run. If you are in a race situation and are reluctant to stop and treat your blister, expect to finish the race in increasing discomfort and be greeted with a pretty nasty sight when you take your socks off.

Like all injuries, prevention is always better than cure and although there is no way to completely protect you from the birth of a blister, there are a number of measures you can take to reduce their regularity and severity.

- **Socks:** By wearing a high quality pair of running socks, you can help to reduce the moisture around your toes and feet, therefore taking away one condition in which blisters thrive. Socks made with a combination of materials such as polyester, nylon and cotton are ideal to wick sweat away from the feet while at the same time make the smooth and reduce friction on the delicate skin.
- **Lubricate:** Covering vulnerable areas such as in between your toes and your heels with a form of lubrication such as petroleum jelly can help to ensure they do not rub together and cause friction, a common cause of blisters.

- **Good shoes:** Well-fitted and well-ventilated shoes that are not tied too tight can also help prevent blisters. By giving your toes enough room to move around freely you can prevent them rubbing against each other. Ventilation also allows your feet to breathe and helps to reduce moisture.

TREATMENT

Try as you might, a blister will get through your defences at one stage or another, so learning how best to treat them is key if you are to keep running pain-free and help the blister heal without risk of infection.

Burst your bubble

There is still much confusion among runners as to whether a blister should be lanced and the fluid drained, or left alone and covered up. The general advice is that if the blister is clear in colour then it can be lanced with a sterilised needle and the fluid drained, but if it is a blood blister, they are often best left alone. In terms of treatment, there is actually little difference between treating a blood blister and a water blister but as a runner, you are more likely to be affected by water blisters, as they are commonly caused by friction on the surface of the skin.

Infection is the main precaution here, so before you burst a blister, make sure the area is well cleaned (ideally by using a medicated/alcohol wipe) and pricked gently with a sterilised needle. Performing this procedure halfway through a run is risky as your chances of infection are far greater. Although it is sometimes the most sensible thing to do if the pressure is causing severe pain, make sure you have all the appropriate implements with you in your first-aid kit before you attempt to lance the blister.

Cover up

Whether you have chosen to lance your blister or simply wish to protect a deeper blood blister, choosing the correct type of plaster can make a big difference – and even help to prevent other blisters. Moleskin plasters, for example, are soft and highly effective at protecting current and preventing future blisters, so once again, make sure you take high-quality blister-specific plasters with you on the trails, as well as having a healthy stash at home.

BLACK TOENAILS

Certainly not exclusive to trail runners, but experienced by most, black toenails are incredibly common and often unavoidable. They are essentially caused by bleeding under the toenails and arise from long runs and or training sessions which feature long downhill sections. As the foot slides forcefully forwards to the front of the shoe on descent, it damages the delicate skin under the nail bed, causing bleeding and, at times, quite significant pain.

The best ways in which you can reduce your chances of black toenails are to wear the right-sized shoes, neither too big, or too small, and to limit the number of extreme descents on your runs. Of course the latter is often not always possible and takes away from the fun of trail running, so the best option is to simply manage the problem if/when it happens. Let pain be your guide and if your toes are too sore to run on, leave off training for a few days – it won't take long for them to heal up. Other than time, there's little you can do to speed up the recovery process.

SKIN ABRASIONS

Any cut to the skin has the potential to become infected, so however you break the skin it's essential you are aware of the risks of skin infections. However unlikely you think an infection will arise following a graze after a fall or an altercation with some brambles, I can tell you that the risk is very real and potentially dangerous. After first-hand experience of an innocent-looking abrasion rapidly turning into cellulitis and resulting in four days on a drip in hospital, I can tell you that it can happen – so be aware of the risks of minor cuts while out on the trails.

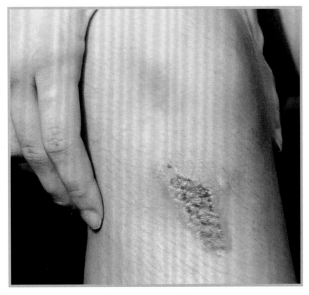

>> *Keep a close eye on skin abrasions*

>> *Black nails can be painful*

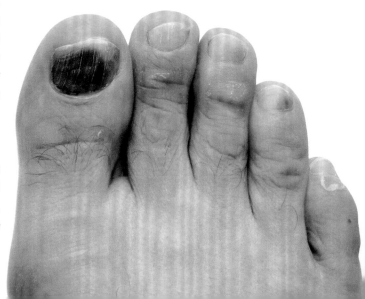

TRAIL FOLIAGE

Perhaps the most potentially dangerous skin abrasions you can acquire are those caused by foliage. Brambles and thorns can cause very serious and very painful skin injuries so, once again, the need to have a well-stocked first-aid kit in your back pack is vital.

Brambles and thorns can often appear from nowhere, so during late summer and autumn runs when they are often at their thickest, be wary of trail paths with dense foliage. If you snag yourself on a branch on either the leg or the torso it's often best to see what damage has been done, and provided there is only a little bleeding, the injury is best and easiest left until you get home. Like blisters, the area should be cleaned thoroughly with an antiseptic wipe. Keep an eye on it for several days – if you notice the area becomes redder, more painful and/or warm to the touch or swollen, make an appointment to see your doctor as soon as possible as the wound has likely become infected and you'll require antibiotics to fight the infection.

13

CHOOSING A TRAIL RACE

The adventure and thrill you can get from running the trails is sometimes enough of an adrenaline rush in itself without you necessarily wanting to race against others. People trail run for a variety of reasons, so if you are attracted to forest or coastal trails as the perfect antidote to the rat race, you shouldn't feel compelled to compete – the trails are there for you to experience, so use them in whichever way you choose to get your fix.

However, even if you initially intended your trail running experience to act as nothing more than escapism, your competitive side might win out and it's only a matter of time before the lure of racing pulls you in.

Assuming you have already put in a fair few miles on the trails before you read this chapter, you'll be well aware of the differences that trail running and road running present. Racing on the trails magnifies that difference. Race tactics, etiquette, kit preparation and attention to route detail are just some of the differences you have to be aware of when trail racing for the first time, so when you're looking for your very first race, it's best to start off easy and build from there.

You can sign up to hundreds of trail races all over the world with distances ranging from a short 10k to 100-mile ultramarathon events, so there's a race for every ability and every appetite for adventure.

YOUR FIRST RACE

When choosing your very first trail race, by far the most important factor to consider is your enjoyment. Although even the longest and hardest races you do you'll enjoy in retrospect, it's really important that you use your first race as part of your trail-running education and enter a race which is a realistic distance for you to complete without too much difficulty. You'll not only enjoy the experience much more, but you'll no doubt get an appetite to enter more trail races in the months and years to come. With this in mind, when you're searching for your first race, make sure:

- you choose terrain you're familiar with;
- the distance is within your means
- you are used to running in the kit required
- the race takes place in familiar conditions
- the scenery is stunning (for race enjoyment)
- reviews of the race confirm that it's ideal for novice/first-time trail racers

For some of the largest organised events, for example the Lakeland Trail Races in the UK (*see* page 206), there will be several choices of distance available to runners, depending on individual levels of ability. So, novice runners can chose to tackle a short 10k trail course or challenge themselves to attempt a half or full marathon.

Preparation for your first race is always key, so when you sign up for the event always read through all of the information the race organisers send you and make sure you have the correct kit for the day of the race. Unlike road races where you can show up in running trousers/shorts and a top, trail races may require that you have certain types of specific kit and navigational equipment, so don't get caught out.

TRAIL RACES WITH A TWIST

In recent years, trail races with a slight difference have grown in popularity, appealing to many people who don't even class themselves as runners. Often of unspecified distance and featuring a range of obstacles, hazards and pyrotechnics, these races offer the perfect balance between the trail-running experience and army-style challenges to tax the mind and body. Such races might not be classed as trail running in the purest sense, but why should that matter? Events such as Tough Mudder (toughmudder.co.uk/toughmudder.com), HellRunner (hellrunner.co.uk) in the UK and Strongman (strongmanrun.nl) in Germany are well worth looking into if you are after a real physical challenge. But remember: training for these events involves more than just running and your preparations should include a series of upper body, lower body and core exercises to ensure you have sufficient strength to pull yourself up, over and through the various obstacles.

TOP TRAIL RACES AROUND THE WORLD

Wherever you live in the world, with just a few clicks of the mouse you'll be able to find a trail event to suit your budget, ability and proximity to your home. As your trail-running career matures and you have entered a few races, grown in confidence and built a fitness level to take on some pretty challenging trails, sooner or later you'll be ready to spread your wings and take on some of the biggest and most popular trail races in the world.

Although not all international races listed here are challenging, my view on entering races overseas is: what's the point in flying halfway around the world to enter a 10k trail race? Trail running is as much about adventure and cherishing the environment as it is about the racing, so if you want to experience a race you'll remember for years to come, make it a long race.

Although Google is always close to hand when you're looking for a race, the following list is a taster of top trail races from around the world you may well want to consider competing in. To make your life easy, I've categorised the races by global territory and given them a difficulty rating:

★	Easy: Ideal for a novice
★ ★	Intermediate: Hard work, but possible if you've been training for months
★ ★ ★	Hard: Best left alone unless you're either nuts or incredibly fit and a highly competent trail runner
★ ★ ★ ★	Insane: You need help! Why would you do that to yourself?

RACE ETIQUETTE

When you become a trail runner, you are automatically accepted as another member of the trail-running family, and like all families we look after each other. Most trail-running events are long distance and in the middle of nowhere, and it's common to pass someone who has fallen, turned an ankle or generally feels unwell. Even though you are racing, **stop and make sure they are okay.** If you've come from the world of road-running races, stopping to help a fellow runner in distress isn't always necessary, as there's often roadside help in some other form. However, on the trails there is no help for miles around, so it's important you show compassion and help someone in trouble. On the whole, the experience of trail running is far more important than the time it takes you to complete the course, so show compassion for your fellow competitors and always lend a hand to someone in trouble.

EUROPE

ERIDGE PARK 10-MILE TRAIL CHALLENGE

Difficulty: ✮

Country: UK

Region/State: Tunbridge Wells, Kent

Distance(s): 16km/10 miles

Climate: September, summer; approx. 15–27°C (59–80°F)

Website: twharriers.org.uk

Description: Voted *Runner's World UK*'s best race in 2009, the Eridge 10 is a hilly and challenging race around a beautiful and private off-road course, and a race that anyone who wants to stake a claim to be a true trail runner should enter. The Eridge Park 10 has everything you'd want in a trail race: mud, hills and is 100 per cent traffic-free. It's a race you can't help but fall in love with and you may well find yourself returning year on year. With one runner quoted as saying "This is what Sunday mornings were made for, excellent race in every department", you'll need a good reason not to sign up for this 10-mile gem.

GREAT TRAIL CHALLENGE

Difficulty: ✮

Country: UK

Region/State: Lake District

Distance(s): 11k or 22k – 7 miles/14miles

Climate: June, summer; approx. 15–23°C (59–73°F)

Website: greattrailchallenge.org

Description: Born in 2012, this new trail event has been set up by the same organisers as the Great North Run – the largest half marathon in Europe. As you'd expect from such a professional outfit, even in its infancy, you can tell this event will grow significantly over time and attract thousands more trail runners to experience some breathtaking Lake District scenery. The Great Trail Challenge is a friendly and un-intimidating event that welcomes

>> *Eridge Park, 10 mile trail challenge*

>> *Great Trail Challenge*

runners of all abilities but who are comfortable on moderately complex trails and, of course, a few tasty (but realistic) inclines. It is a great place to begin your trail racing career.

BROOKS HELLRUNNER

Difficulty: ★ ☆ ☆ ☆

Country: UK

Region/State: North, middle and south of England

Distance(s): approx. 16km/10 miles

Climate: November, winter; approx. 0–10°C (32–50°F)

Website: hellrunner.co.uk

Description: How could you not be intrigued by a race which features something called The Bog of Doom? Ten glorious miles of British countryside, with the bog of doom thrown in for good measure, will test your trail-running skills and your willingness to have a whole lot of fun. Pyrotechnics, disco music and a carnival atmosphere make HellRunner a challenging but fun and uncompetitive trail race. If you *do* want to race that's fine, but most people simply enter for a great time... and to find out just what this Bog of Doom is...

>> *Brooks Hellrunner*

LAKELAND TRAILS

Difficulty: ★
Country: UK
Region/State: Lake District
Distance(s): 10k, 18k, Half marathon and marathon
Climate: Different races organised throughout the year; 5–23°C (41–73°F)
Website: lakelandtrails.org
Description: Generally recognised as one of the UK's most scenic series of trail runs, Lakeland Trails races are set in the stunning Lake District on un-complex trails and bridle paths. With thousands of runners taking part in the wide range of trail races spread throughout the year, it is the perfect event and location for beginners and experienced runners alike. The combination of the stunning views and the friendly atmosphere has helped to grow this event from just 80 competitors in 2004 to over 10,000 in 2012.

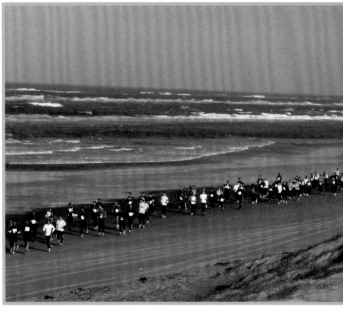

>> Egmond Half Marathon

EGMOND HALF MARATHON

Difficulty: ★ ★
Country: Netherlands
Region/State: Bergen
Distance(s): 21km/13 miles
Climate: January, winter; approx. 1–5°C (33–41°F)
Website: egmondhalvemarathon.nl
Description: With around 15,000 runners taking part every year, the Egmond Half Marathon is one mass participation event you should seriously consider signing up for. Run in the winter, often in heavy snow (the event was actually cancelled in 2010 due to the snow being too severe), this trail race is certainly not for the faint-hearted. With sections of the race run on the beach and sand dunes, you can guarantee this January race will put any thermal or windbreaker jacket to the test – as well as your mental toughness. The final 2k will also push you to your limits. Why? Why not find out yourself. If you like a challenge, you'll love the Egmond Half Marathon.

>> Lakeland Trails

GRIZZLY

Difficulty: ★ ★ ☆ ☆
Country: UK
Region/State: Devon
Distance(s): 32km/20 miles
Climate: March, Early spring; approx. 5–10°C (41–50°F)
Website: axevalleyrunners.org.uk
Description: The only bad thing about this race is that there are only 1,800 places available, which is a shame because thousands more are denied the chance to run this brilliant 20-miler. The Grizzly is officially described as "twentyish, muddy, hilly, boggy, beachy miles of the multiest-terrain running experience" and is arguably one of the most popular off-road running events in the UK. Elite-runner free, the Grizzly attracts runners who simply love trail running and are looking for a fun race to get dirty in (thigh-deep mud makes sure of that) and the opportunity to take in some sensational views of the south coast of England. Family friendly and with the chance to get hosed down by the local fire brigade after the race, this event is a must. It's not easy, but boy, is it fun! Sign up quickly – places are snapped up fast.

KÖNIGSSCHLÖSSER ROMANTIK MARATHON

Difficulty: ★ ★ ☆ ☆
Country: Germany
Region/State: Bavaria
Distance(s): Marathon
Climate: July, summer; approx. 18–26°C (64–79°F)
Website: koenigludwigmarathon.de
Description: A beautiful 26.2-mile trail run with beautiful castles and forests as a backdrop, this race is long and hard – but the scenery will quickly make it all worthwhile. A great race for competitive runners as well as novices, this fairly small event (800 runners) is intimate and one which you will never, ever forget. With the stunning course being reasonably flat, it's a perfect chance to clock up a fast time if you like, or simply enjoy the views and inhale the sweet Bavarian air on an un-complex and soft trail route.

MITTENWALD

Difficulty: ★ ★ ☆ ☆
Country: Germany
Region/State: Bavaria
Distance(s): 11km/7 miles
Climate: July, summer; approx. 13–24°C (55–75°F)
Website: laufclub-mittenwald.de
Description: Just to the north of the German border with Austria lies the stunningly beautiful town of Mittenwald. Beginning in the town itself, this 11km race puts those hill training sessions to the test as you embark on a steep climb totalling 1,425m by the time you reach the finish line. A fast race this is not, but a steep and challenging one it certainly is – pushing your lactic acid tolerance to the limits. Your hard work will be rewarded, though, with a pasta and beer party for all finishers! A great event if you enjoy the hills and appreciate some of the best views the Alps can offer.

TOUGH MUDDER

Difficulty: ★ ★
Country: UK, Germany, Australia and USA
Region/State: Several locations throughout the world
Distance(s): 16–19km/10–12 miles
Climate: Spring/summer; approx. 13–20+°C (55–68+°F)
Website: toughmudder.co.uk
Description: Arguably one of the most popular obstacle races in the world, you can sign up for Tough Mudder events at several locations in the UK, Germany, Australia and USA. There are many ways to describe what Tough Mudder events are all about, but the organisers explain it better than anyone: "Triathlons, marathons and other mud runs are more stressful than fun. Not Tough Mudder. At Tough Mudder, we meet you at the finish line with a pint and a live band. It's pretty hard to take yourself seriously when you're covered in mud and have just finished an obstacle called 'Just The Tip', so please don't show up at a Tough Mudder without a sense of humour." Enough said really.

If you want to push your upper and lower body, and cardiovascular strength, sign up for Tough Mudder.

>> *Tough Mudder*

THE DRAGON'S BACK RACE™

Difficulty: ★ ★ ★ ★
Country: Wales, UK
Region/State: Central-east Wales
Distance(s): 320k/200 miles over 5 days
Climate: June, summer (though times are variable); approx. 14–18+°C (57–64+°F)
Website: dragonsbackrace.com
Description: If you are considering running this race, it's likely you already know something about it and what a challenge it is. Wales's answer to the Marathon des Sables (the Sahara Marathon, the Toughest Race on Earth) is one heck of an undertaking and will take many months to prepare for. Running 320km in 5 days across Wales isn't something you do on a whim and although running in Wales in autumn is likely to offer you some of the best views in the world, don't consider taking this race on unless you've been trail running for several years. Hilly, potentially muddy, a huge test of human endurance, but with stunning scenery – this race has it all!

USA AND CANADA
BIG SUR MUD RUN

Difficulty: ★
Country: USA
Region/State: California
Distance(s): 8k/5 miles
Climate: Spring /early summer; approx. 15–20+°C (50–68+°F)
Website: bsim.org
Description: Short and sweet it may be, but this race will push you to your limits. With mud and obstacles galore, the Big Sur Mud Run is great fun to compete in and will have you coming back for more every year. With a mixture of hills, mud and a series of military-style obstacles, this 5-miler will feel more like twice that distance by the time you reach

>> *The Dragon's Back Race*

>> *Big Sur Mud Run*

the finish line, so don't let the short course lead you into a false sense of security.

DIPSEA
Difficulty: ⭐
Country: US
Region/State: California
Distance(s): 12km / 8 miles
Climate: June, summer; approx. 10–15°C (50–59°F)
Website: dipsea.org
Description: Claimed to be the oldest trail race in America, its history alone should make you want to take part in this fantastic Californian event. Starting from Mill Valley and finishing at Stinson Beach, the Dipsea is considered to be one of the most beautiful courses in the world. This 12km race takes you up to a height of 1,360ft on ravine trails and steps, giving you wonderful views of the surrounding area. As well as its location and scenery, the unique attraction about this is race is its handicapped system, giving anyone young or old a chance to win the event. With a limit of 1,500 runners, this event is intimate but one certainly worth entering if you want to taste a bit of trail running history.

ROMANCING THE ISLAND
Difficulty: ⭐
Country: USA
Region/State: California
Distance(s): 12km/25km
Climate: March, early spring; approx. 12–17°C (53–63°F)
Website: envirosports.com
Description: How could you not be interested in signing up for a trail race with the Golden Gate Bridge and the island of Alcatraz as a backdrop? The Romancing the Island trail race is a small but hugely popular event, which loops around Angel Island (twice for those choosing the 25km distance), giving runners stunning views of San Francisco for

the entire race. With a good trail surface and only a 500ft ascent, this race is great for those new to trail running and the perfect excuse to holiday in San Francisco.

RUN FOR THE TOAD
Difficulty: ☆
Country: Canada
Region/State: Ontario
Distance(s): 25km/50km
Climate: October, autumn; approx. 12–17°C (43–57°F)
Website: runforthetoad.com
Description: One of Ontario's most popular trail races, this family friendly event is a fantastic day out and epitomises everything that recreational trail running should be. With the choice of a 25km or a 50km course, Run for the Toad is a race for mixed abilities that takes you on soft trails through the forest. Not the most challenging of events in Canada, but arguably one of the friendliest.

RUN TO THE CLOUDS
Difficulty: ☆
Country: Canada
Region/State: Vancouver
Distance(s): 10.5/13.5/25km
Climate: March, early spring; approx. 5–15°C (41–59°F)
Website: clubfatass.com/events/RunToTheClouds
Description: With a name like Run to the Clouds, you'd expect a hilly race which gives you access to some stunning Canadian scenery... and thankfully there are no disappointments. With a climb of over 2,000ft for the 25km course, the predominantly gravel trails not only take you to the clouds but provide you with captivating views of the Buntzen Lake and the Greater Vancouver area.

IMOGENE PASS RUN
Difficulty: ☆ ☆
Country: USA
Region/State: Colorado
Distance(s): 27km/17.1 miles
Climate: September, autumn; approx. 5–20°C (41–68°F)
Website: imogenerun.com
Description: Races evolving over time are often the best to race in and the Imogene Pass Run is no exception. Starting life back in 1974 with just six runners, it has now grown to a 1,500-competitor event and attracts runners from all over the world. Run in late summer, the conditions can make the race one you'll always remember for right or wrong reasons, so be prepared for every type of weather Mother Nature can throw at you. Run on 4 x 4 tracks, the trail is tough but well within the means of fairly new trail runners – despite the tasty ascent. With a total climb of 1,617m and a decent of 1,330m this 17-mile race has a good mixture of up and downhill and will test your resolve to the very end. This is a great race for anyone wanting to experience the trails of the western USA.

NAPA VALLEY 10K/HALF/FULL MARATHON
Difficulty: ☆ ☆
Country: USA
Region/State: California
Distance(s): 10km / 21.1k / 42.2 km – 6.2 miles/ half marathon / marathon
Climate: March, spring; approx. 12–17°C (53–63°F)
Website: envirosports.com
Description: Another gem of a trail race in the Bothe-Napa Valley State Park in the state of California, the Napa Valley series of 10k, half marathon or marathon events is a serious test of your trail-running skills. With a trail surface significantly more complex than that of 'Romancing the Island' in Angel Island State park, the combination of streams, rocks and

inclines makes this a race you'll have to work for, but the reward of finishing makes it all worthwhile. With a total climb of approximately 1,000ft, 2,000ft and 3,000ft for the 10k, half marathon and marathon respectively, the hills certainly keep your legs interested for whichever distance you choose – but what better tonic than the views that await you? Spaces are limited so sign up quickly.

MOOSE MOUNTAIN TRAIL RACES
Difficulty: ☆ ☆ ☆
Country: Canada
Region/State: Alberta
Distance(s): 42km / marathon
Climate: August, summer; approx. 14–21°C (57–70°F)
Website: moosetrailraces.com
Description: A marathon with quintessential views of the Canadian mountains... need I say more? Starting at the base of the Rockies and finishing 42km later, 3,000ft higher with views that will take your breath away, this marathon is arguably one of Canada's most spectacular and one which should certainly be on your to do list if you find yourself in Alberta. Although often a little muddy at the start, the logging roads and mountain trails will take you on a Canadian adventure that will test your legs, lungs and mental toughness, but certainly cement your love of the trails.

PIKES PEAK MARATHON
Difficulty: ☆ ☆ ☆
Country: USA
Region/State: Colorado
Distance(s): 42.2km / marathon
Climate: August, summer; approx. 4–27°C (40–81°F)
Website: pikespeakmarathon.org
Description: I very nearly awarded the Pikes Peak Marathon a rating of 4 stars, but as it's only a mere 26.2 mile race, I figured that a rating of 3 stars was about right – just. This is a tough race and should only be taken on if you have got some serious mountain mileage under your belt. The beginning of the race might seem like any other marathon, but when you consider that in the first 10 miles alone, you'll be climbing over 6,000ft, you soon realise that this is perhaps one of the hardest marathons you'll ever run. Although the trail surface is not challenging in itself, the extremes of climate (it may well snow) and the climb make this a serious event for up to 700 serious trail runners.

WESTERN STATES 100-MILE ENDURANCE RUN
Difficulty: ☆ ☆ ☆ ☆
Country: USA
Region/State: California
Distance(s): 160km/100 miles
Climate: June, summer; approx. 15–23+°C (59–73+°F)
Website: wser.org
Description: This a serious trail race for serious runners looking for a seriously tough race. Won by Scott Jurek a record seven times in a row, the fastest time of which was an incredible 15 hours 36 minutes, the Western States 100 is a brutal test of your physical and mental strength. Climbing over 18,000ft and descending 23,000ft over the course of the race, this trail event throws everything endurance running can possibly throw at you – and more. Unless you have made it, or plan to make it, your life-long ambition to run this race, do not even consider entering unless you have spent years preparing for it.

AUSTRALIA AND NEW ZEALAND
JUMBO-HOLDSWORTH TRAIL RACE
Difficulty: ☆
Country: New Zealand
Region/State: Wellington, Tararua Forest Park
Distance(s): 12–24km/7–14 miles

>> *Jumbo-Holdsworth Trail Race*

Climate: January, summer; approx. 14–20°C (57–68°F)

Website: techs.net.nz/trusthouse.co.nz/sport/mountain

Description: Dubbed 'The premier mountain race in the Wairarapa', this attractive trail race is perfect for novice runners and a great introduction to what trail racing is all about. With a choice between the short course (12km) or the long course (24km), there is something for all abilities at this race. Far from being an easy race (the hills make sure of that), the trails are not overly complex and as you'd expect from any trail race in New Zealand, the views make up for that lactic acid burn.

ROTORUA OFF-ROAD HALF MARATHON

Difficulty: ★

Country: New Zealand

Region/State: Rotorua

Distance(s): 21km/13.1 miles

Climate: March, late summer; approx. 12–20°C (54–68°F)

Website: eventpromotions.co.nz

>> *Rotorua Off-road Half Marathon*

Description: A great family day out, the Rotorua Off-Road Half Marathon is ideal for runners with families. With a 5 and 10k race available for mums, dads and kids not quite ready to tackle the half marathon course, this event is perfect to show what a fantastic community trail racers are. The main half marathon course is run through the spectacular Whakarewarewa Forest. It's a two-lap course, taking in scenic trails and smooth gravel forest roads, and with around 1,500–2,000 competitors taking part every year, the atmosphere is fun, inviting and will no doubt make you want to come back for more year on year. Without extreme hills or trail complexity, it is ideal if you're new to trail running, so get signed up and look forward to treating the family to a great day out.

SYDNEY TRAILRUNNING SERIES
Difficulty: ✮
Country: Australia
Region/State: New South Wales
Distance(s): Various distances
Climate: All year round
Website: mountainsports.com.au
Description: This series of trail races in and around Sydney is a must if you have recently started taking to the trails and want to get a taste of what trail running in Australia is all about. With an event suitable for all levels of ability, these races are made for newcomers or those wishing to test their speed on un-complex but attractive trails. With events spread throughout the year in locations ranging from Manly to Bobbin Head, there's no excuse not to get involved, so check out the website and register your interest.

AUSTRALIAN OUTBACK MARATHON
Difficulty: ✮ ✮
Country: Australia
Region/State: Central Australia, Ayers Rock

>> *Australian Outback Marathon*

Distance(s): 42km (26.2 miles) (other distances are also available)
Climate: July, winter; approx. 22+°C (73+°F)
Website: australianoutbackmarathon.com
Description: Any runner who gets his or her lifeblood from trail-running scenery will find it very difficult not to be seduced by the Outback Marathon. The most iconic landmark in Australia, Uluru (Ayers Rock) serves as the perfect backdrop for this hot and dusty outback 26.2-mile race and every year runners from all over the world come to race in this most spiritual and challenging marathon. With supplementary distances for those not quite ready to tackle a full marathon, this outback race is definitely one for the

>> *The Goat Adventure Run*

memory bank and one that provides you with views no other trail event could get close to offering. Do it!

THE GOAT ADVENTURE RUN

Difficulty: ⭐ ⭐
Country: New Zealand
Region/State: Tongariro National Park
Distance(s): 21km/half marathon
Climate: December, summer; approx. 8–16°C (46–61°F)
Website: thegoat.co.nz
Description: A rugged adventure trail run in Tongariro National Park, a World Heritage Site, provides the perfect way to see this beautiful part of New Zealand. A challenging 1,000m+ vertical ascent over 21km on every different type of trail surface you can think of, The Goat will give you an incredibly diverse range of sights, from lava flows to cascading waterfalls. The terrain and sights epitomise New Zealand and with only 600 places available, the event usually sells out in less than three days. Experience and an above average level of fitness are recommended, but if you have successfully raced on similar trails this race should not overwhelm you. If you can climb hilly trails and you have grit, this race is well within your means.

MT GLORIOUS MOUNTAIN TRAILS
Difficulty: ★ ★
Country: Australia
Region/State: Queensland
Distance(s): 22km / half marathon
Climate: February, late summer; approx. 16–24°C (61–75°F)
Website: runtrails.org/articles/events/glorious
Description: With a climb of 1,200m in 22km, in often very warm conditions, make sure you're well prepared if you sign up for this race. As beautiful as it is, the Mt Glorious Mountain Trails race certainly deserves some respect. Although the 22km distance is not insurmountable for those fairly new to trail running, the heat and climb makes life pretty unpleasant for you if you do not have the experience or fitness to handle the course, so only enter if you are in good shape and love hills. Small (approximately 150 spaces) and family friendly, this race just outside Brisbane is a great challenge for the improver trail runner and worth looking into for a fun, but exhausting, day out.

ROUTEBURN CLASSIC
Difficulty: ★ ★
Country: New Zealand
Region/State: The Divide, Glenorchy
Distance(s): 32km/20 miles
Climate: April, autumn; approx. 12–20°C (54–68°F)
Website: goodtimesevents.net
Description: As soon as you find out this race is run over 32km, in a National Park, inside a World Heritage Area in Fiordland, you don't need to be told how stunning the scenery is. A race for fairly experienced runners and those who will relish the climb to 1,127m above sea level, the Routeburn Classic is an adventure race which has true adventure characteristics for the entire distance. With the potential for some seriously wet and wild weather, runners should be well prepared for

>> *Routeburn Classic*

all types of weather on race day – but should the sun shine, you are in for a real treat. Typical New Zealand postcard views await you throughout the Routeburn, so if you've got the legs and lungs to see you through 32km, do yourself a favour and sign up for this 350-place race.

TOUGH BLOKE CHALLENGE
Difficulty: ★ ★
Country: Australia
Region/State: NSW and Victoria

Distance(s): 7km/4 miles, including several obstacles
Climate: March and June, autumn/winter; approx. 12–18°C (54–64°F)
Website: toughblokechallenge.com.au
Description: Fast growing in popularity in Australia and New Zealand, the Tough Bloke Challenge series of races is the perfect blend of trails, hills, obstacles, mud and fun. Racing to win is not the philosophy here, rather a test of your team work and ability to push yourself up and over some tough obstacles, often requiring some help from fellow racers is what these races are all about. The Tough Bloke Challenges are often best if you get a group of mates together and enter as part of a team. Beers afterwards will never taste better. Another series of similar events you might like to consider in New Zealand are Tough Guy and Gal – find more information at toughguyandgirl.co.nz.

SIX FOOT TRACK MARATHON
Difficulty: ★ ★ ★
Country: Australia
Region/State: Blue Mountains
Distance(s): 42km / marathon
Climate: March, early autumn; approx. 12–20°C (54–68°F)
Website: sixfoot.com
Description: Australia's fifth largest marathon and by far the country's largest off-road marathon, this event will capture your heart as you race across the beautiful Blue Mountains just outside Sydney. However, do not let the picturesque backdrop of Australia's most beautiful mountain range lull you into thinking that this will be a sightseeing marathon. The race is brutal, and with the averaging finishing time being 5:30 hours, you know it's not going to be quick. The climbs may be tough and the conditions likely to be warm, but the world-renowned Six Foot Track Marathon attracts runners from all over the world – so if you fancy a challenge and want to be one of the lucky 850 entrants, get signed up now.

LARK HILL DUSK TO DAWN
Difficulty: ★ ★ ★ ★
Country: Australia
Region/State: Western Australia
Distance(s): 50k/100k – 31 / 62 miles
Climate: March, late summer; approx. 18+°C (64+°F)
Website: aura.asn.au/LarkHill.html
Description: Not for the faint-hearted, this is one seriously hard race for which you must be incredibly fit, or ever so slightly mad, to even consider

entering! With the choice of running the 50k or the 100k course, this looped event is not taxing in terms of inclines or navigational skills, but purely a test of physical and mental endurance. With good amenities and plenty of places to refuel and rehydrate, this is a great race for anyone interested in ultra-trail running and/or with a view of racing in more extreme events over the coming years.

REST OF THE WORLD
CUBAN TRAIL MARATHON
Difficulty: ★ ★
Country: Cuba
Region/State: Sierra Maestra
Distance(s): 42.2k (26.2 miles)

Climate: February, winter; approx. 16–21°C (61–70°F)
Website: 209events.com/event.php? event=67
Description: This is not the largest trail race in the world, but the warm reception you'll receive all the way around this marathon certainly makes it one of the friendliest. Run in warm conditions and on a mixture of forest trails and dirt roads, this marathon will give you some stunning views of this Caribbean island and you'll be cheered on all the way round by locals. Although the climate might make the going pretty tough if you're not acclimatised to warm weather running, this event can easily be completed if you have a good level of fitness and you have prepared well for long runs.

>> *Cuban Trail Marathon*

>> *Fuji Mountain Race*

closer. The final stages of the race become steeper and with loose rock under foot you'll be fighting to find your grip – as well as your breath. With other distanced races also available, there is something for everyone at this event.

GREAT WALL MARATHON
Difficulty: ★ ★
Country: China
Region/State: Beijing
Distance(s): 42km/marathon (other distances available)
Climate: July; approx., summer 0–40°C (32–104°F)
Website: great-wall-marathon.com

FUJI MOUNTAIN RACE
Difficulty: ★ ★
Country: Japan
Region/State: Yamanashi
Distance(s): 21k/13k – half marathon or 7 miles
Climate: July; approx, summer. 0–24°C (32–75°F)
Website: city.fujiyoshida.yamanashi.jp/div/english/html/race.html
Description: If being one of 2,500 people running up a 13-mile mountain trail in Japan doesn't whet your appetite for trail racing then nothing will. Trail and adventure runners have been enjoying this hugely popular race to the top of one of Japan's most iconic volcanic peaks since 1948. With the prospect of climbing 3,000m in 13 miles, runners can expect a true challenge as they run for over 2 hours through changing conditions – from 24°C at the start to zero near the summit. This race is a true trail challenge, as the terrain changes from fairly standard trails initially and gradually becomes more complex as the finishing line and summit get

>> *Great Wall Marathon*

Description: A trail race with a difference, the Great Wall Marathon was started in 1999 and has fast become an incredibly popular race. With over 2,000 runners from 50 countries, the Great Wall Marathon is a truly international event and is one race any marathon runner should seriously consider entering. With a 7.5km race also available, this is an event which the entire family could enjoy – but don't expect an easy race. Run in hot and humid conditions and over an undulating course, this race is tough, so be well prepared.

THE OTTER AFRICAN TRAIL RUN
Difficulty: ✭ ✭
Country: South Africa
Region/State: Cape Town
Distance(s): 42km (marathon)
Climate: September; approx. 12–20°C (54–68°F)

>> *The Otter African Trail Run*

Website: theotter.co.za
Description: Dubbed a trail runner's dream, the Otter Trail Run is a 42km race on the southern coast of South Africa through the beautiful Tsitsikamma National Park. As trail marathons go, the Otter Run is not the most challenging on the circuit, so it is certainly one to consider if you want to take part in an easy(ish) race and not be too exhausted to enjoy the beautiful views this part of the world offers. A total ascent of 2,500m certainly makes sure you are kept on your toes, and combined with the varied trail surface of rock faces, sand and pebble beaches, you'll get a huge amount of variety from this race. Expect warm conditions for the race, but above all enjoy the views which await you – this is what trail running in South Africa is all about.

HOUT BAY TRAIL CHALLENGE
Difficulty: ✭ ✭ ✭
Country: South Africa
Region/State: Cape Town
Distance(s): 36km (22.4 miles)
Climate: July; approx. 12–18°C (54–64°F)
Website: www.houtbaychallenge.co.za
Description: This raw trail race is the ultimate trail running test. The Hout Bay Trail Challenge will challenge your endurance, you hill running ability and also your navigational skills. Organisers have made it mandatory to carry the right gear with you throughout the race, along with the correct food and drink to see you safely round the 36km of mountain trails. With the opportunity to take part as an individual or as part of a team, this race is perfect for a range of abilities – despite its many physical and technical challenges. With the iconic Table Mountain as a backdrop, the Hout Bay Trail Challenge is set in a beautiful part of South Africa, so although it is claimed to be one of the toughest races in South Africa, at least the stunning views help to ease the pain.

>> *Safaricom Marathon*

SAFARICOM MARATHON

Difficulty: ★ ★ ★
Country: Kenya
Region/State: Nairobi
Distance(s): 42.2 miles / marathon
Climate: June; approx 16–24°C (61–75°F)
Website: tusk.org

Description: A true safari marathon 140 miles north of Nairobi, the Safaricom Marathon is a trail race showing you the true beauty of Africa. Set in Lewa Wildlife Conservancy, this trail marathon takes you on a wild journey, with breathtaking views of Mount Ololokwe and Mount Kenya. It's rare you get the chance to safely run in the same playground as wild animals such as zebra, giraffe and buffalo, but this is exactly what awaits you when you take your place on the starting line of the Safaricom Marathon. With the peace of mind that helicopters and planes circling above you provide, ensuring that there is no threat to your safety from wildlife, this is a rare opportunity to experience wild Africa at its best. Run at altitude, this race is far from easy but, all things considered, it's one you should put on your wish list.

ATACAMA CROSSING

Difficulty: ★ ★ ★ ★
Country: Chile
Region/State: Andes
Distance(s): 250km / 155 miles in six stages
Climate: July; approx. 0–40°C (32–104°F)
Website: 4deserts.com/atacamacrossing

Description: The Atacama Crossing forms part of the 4 Deserts Marathon Challenge and is arguably one of the most beautiful of the four. An incredibly taxing event for mind, body and spirit, this 250km race will not only test you by taking you to 4,000m, but the complex trails and extremes of temperature

>> *Atacama Crossing*

make this race a true test of durability. For the duration of the race you will have to be self-sufficient and carry everything from food and drink to first aid supplies – needless to say this race is reserved only for the most experienced of trail/adventure racers. One of those challenge of a lifetime events, the Atacama Crossing will push you to your limits and beyond – but the experience and memories will stay with you for a lifetime.

COPPER CANYON RUN

Difficulty: ✫ ✫ ✫ ✫
Country: Mexico
Region/State: Sierra Madre
Distance(s): 83 km/51 miles
Climate: March, spring; approx. 25+°C (77+°F)

Website: caballoblanco.com
Description: Hot, arid, complex and very long: four reasons that this event has been rated four stars. This mysterious part of the world was popularised by the running legend who formed part of this book's introduction. Micah True ran many miles in this part of the world, and following his tragic passing, the race is now run with him very much in mind. An incredibly tough race for runners even of exceptional ability, the Copper Canyon Run is one of those events which you should earmark and spend years training for. The challenging terrain and hot conditions make this race far tougher than its 51 miles might suggest, so race-specific training is essential if you are tempted to put your name down for this incredibly beautiful but difficult trail event.

INDEX